Strategic Classroom Design
Creating an Environment for Flexible Learning

JESSICA MARTIN

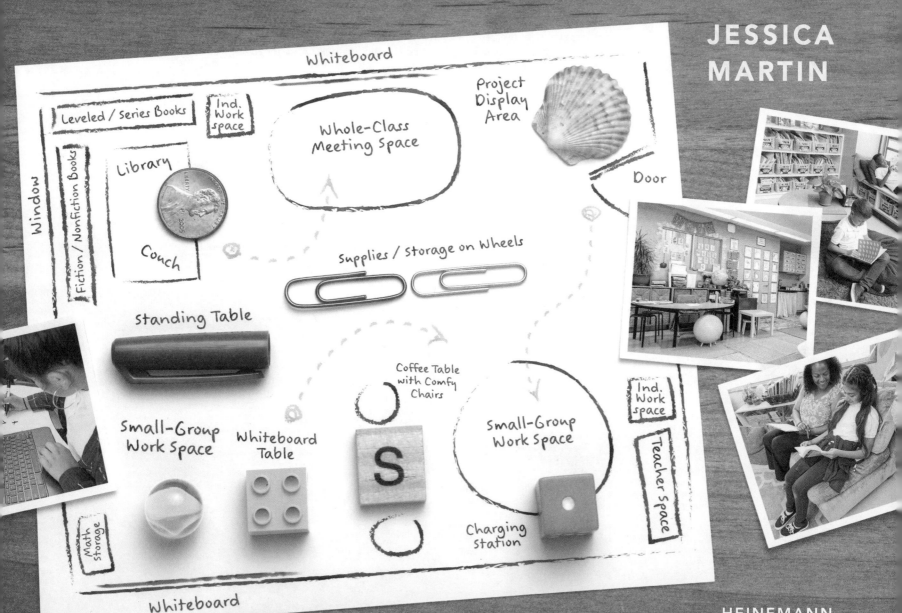

Whiteboard

Leveled / Series Books

Ind. Work space

Whole-Class Meeting Space

Project Display Area

Window

Fiction / Nonfiction Books

Library

Couch

Door

Supplies / Storage on Wheels

Standing Table

Small-Group Work Space

Whiteboard Table

Coffee Table with Comfy Chairs

Small-Group Work Space

Ind. Work space

Teacher Space

Math storage

Charging Station

Whiteboard

HEINEMANN
Portsmouth, NH

Heinemann

361 Hanover Street

Portsmouth, NH 03801–3912

www.heinemann.com

Offices and agents throughout the world

The author and publisher wish to thank those who have generously given permission to reprint borrowed material:

Book cover of *Paragraphs for Middle School: A Sentence-Composing Approach* by Donald and Jenny Killgallon. Copyright © 2013 by Donald and Jenny Killgallon. Reprinted by permission of Heinemann.

Library of Congress Cataloging-in-Publication Data

Names: Martin, Jessica (Educational consultant), author.
Title: Strategic classroom design : creating an environment for flexible
   learning / by Jessica Martin.
Description: Portsmouth, NH : Heinemann, [2020] | Includes bibliographical
   references.
Identifiers: LCCN 2019028699 | ISBN 9780325109152 (paperback)
Subjects: LCSH: Classroom environment. | Open learning.
Classification: LCC LB3013 .M37 2019 | DDC 371.102/4—dc23
LC record available at https://lccn.loc.gov/2019028699

Acquisition Editor: Holly Kim Price
Production Editor: Kimberly Capriola
Cover and interior Designer: Suzanne Heiser
Cover and interior spot photos: Michael Grover
Typesetter: Suzanne Heiser
Manufacturing: Steve Bernier

Printed in the United States of America on acid-free paper

24 23 22 21 20   VP   1 2 3 4 5

for

My folks: Cheryn and Ron, Verna and Reginald

My heart: Tylia, Nathan, Jada, and Nico

My love: Jonathan

Contents

Acknowledgments

With Gratitude

Playing the game of basketball since the age of eight has taught me a lot about the importance of practice, persistence, sacrifice, and teamwork. I am so grateful to have had the opportunity to learn the game early on as it also has many life lessons. I am also grateful for the opportunity to collaborate with teams both on and off the court that have looked to get everyone involved, worked efficiently toward a common goal, and provided compassion and encouragement in the midst of difficulty. I have always felt most comfortable with a team around me. Like basketball, I have come to realize that, for me, teaching is also a team sport.

This book would not be possible without the teams I have been fortunate to be part of. These teams were mostly filled with strong women from diverse backgrounds. They taught me about balance, patience, and how to reframe challenges as opportunities. I am forever grateful.

My Rookie Season

Team Lawndale

Thank you to all of my teammates at Billy Mitchell Elementary in Lawndale, California, and most especially the team that helped me navigate my first years of teaching: Alice Acevedo, Laura Bradley, Norma Bridges, Jenifer Briggs, Evelyn Chidsey, Donna Chisolm, Cheryl Chobanian, Donna Patton, Pamela Madera, Gerda Schmidt, Martha Shaw, Sidney Shyer, Merle Templeton, Shannon Wilkins, and Roberta Wynn.

A big thank-you to Juan Ruiz, one of the hardest working and resourceful plant managers you could ever hope to work with.

A very special thank-you my dear friend, Judy Sartor, who mentored me through my first few years of teaching and beyond.

Midseason Trade

Team UCLA Lab School

Thank you to all of my teammates at the UCLA Lab School, most especially those who supported me during my transition to becoming a demonstration teacher: Raul Alarcon, Hasmik Avetisian, Ileana Barberena, Laurette Cano, Nancy Chakravarty, Jan Cohn, Susan DeBlasio, Ava De La Sota, Naty Elli-Drennon, Kent Gardiner, Greta Gebhardt, Dana Giglia, Joyce Friedman, Margaret Heritage, Sara Hernandez, Dr. Muriel Ifekwunigwe, Judith Kantor, Tonya Leija, Doris Levy, Ruthellen Moss, Jean Miyamoto, Susan Oswald, Marie Parks, George Parks, Jan Powell, Laurie Ramirez, Erma Riley, Alejandra Rivera, Lisa Rosenthal Schaffer, Norma Silva, Vicki Silva, Don Steiner, Sharon Sutton, and the lovely Nancy Williams.

A special thank-you to Dr. Megan Franke for her guidance, patience, and encouragement to always take time to reflect on my practice.

I am especially grateful to Julie Kern Schwerdtfeger for being such a munificent first teaching partner. I hit the jackpot the day I was partnered with you!

The Playoffs

Team TCRWP

Thank you to all of my teammates at the Teachers College Reading and Writing Project, and most especially to those who encouraged me during my first few years as a new staff developer: Amber Boyd, Maurie Brooks, Denise Capasso, Grace Cho, Mary-Ann Colbert, M. Colleen Cruz, Emily DeLiddo, Colleen Dougherty, Kim Ethun, Katie Even, Ian Fleischer, Jane Bean-Folkes, Gravity Goldberg, Christine Holley, Tasha Kalista, Mara Kaunitz, Wairimu Kiambuthi, Alison Kilts, Timothy Lopez, Natalie Louis, Tom Marshall, Marjorie Martinelli, Enid Martinez, Ami Metha, Mary Ann Mustac, Beth Neville, Kathy Neville, Marika Pàez Wiesen, Stephanie Parsons, Sarah Picard Taylor, Cia Pinkerton, Bibinaz Pirayesh, Rob Ross, Jennifer Serravallo, Karma Suttles, Hannah Schneewind, Emily Butler Smith, Shanna Schwartz, Ray Smith, Ruth Swinney, Joe Yukish, and Jory Zand.

I feel especially fortunate to have the opportunity to know and work alongside Katherine Bomer, Kathy Collins, Mary Ehrenworth, Amanda Hartman, Laurie Pessah, Kathleen Tolan, and the incomparable Lucy Calkins. I'd like to thank them for their heartfelt leadership and wisdom. Each has influenced my thinking beyond measure and continues to inspire new hope in all that is beautiful and possible within our classroom spaces.

The Expansion Organization
Team Growing Educators

For their commitment to teachers, students, and families, I would like to thank my past and present teammates at Growing Educators: Angela Bae, Michelle Bamrick Petersen, April Browning, Erin Donelson, Angela Dyborn, Audrey Fann Ellis, Courtney Farrell, Julia Fernandez, Karin Figueroa, Barbara Goodwin, Casey Gruber, Natalia Huezo, Regina Hurh Kim, Genie Hwang, Nancy Infante, Jodi Manby, Brenda Meza, Cristina Navarro-Aguirre, Jamaica Ross, Beverly Sanchez, Krissia Self, Adriana Sheinbaum, Ana Torres, Shanna Trombetta, Claudia Vecchio Wille, and Shelly Warshauer.

For sharing their skill, time, and talent with our organization, many thanks as well to Michelle Baldonado, Candis Berens, Joyce Friedman, Heather Hall, Cory Hills, Courtney Hull, Yuri Leon, Anjali Ryan, Antonio Sacre, Laurenne Sala, Cathy Skubik, and Logan Williams.

I'd also like to thank the brilliant Renee Houser for her part in the genesis and early development of this book. What a journey we had together. I have learned so much from you, dear friend.

The Affiliate Squads
Team School Communities

For welcoming us to try out strategic classroom design elements in classrooms across the city, thank you to the teams of educators at Woodcrest Elementary, South Park Elementary, and Harry Bridges K–8 Span School, all of LAUSD; New Heights Charter school of LAUSD; Alvarado Elementary, Jackie Robinson Academy, and Webster Avenue Elementary, all of LBUSD; and R. H. Dana Middle School of the Wiseburn Unified School District.

A special thank-you to the current and former administrators of these schools: Amy Berfield, Dr. Tina Choyce, Kiana Clark, Sarah Forrester, Kery Jackson, Lou Mardesich, Dr. Damita Myers-Miller, Dr. Lucy Salazar, and Dennis Schaefer.

Team Teacher Collaborators

I am so appreciative of Khalia Benjamin, Shayla Brown, Christine Chavez, Aimee Glotz, Julia Fernandez, Courtney Hull, Tina Marraccini, Beverly Sanchez, and Lori Yoshizaki for all of the work they've done and continue to do with co-creating spaces that nurture, support connectedness, and advocate for collaboration. What a gift each of you are to this profession!

I am especially grateful to Rosanne López for making classroom design a priority. Stepping into a learning space she creates is like taking a much-needed breath of fresh air. Simply amazing!

I couldn't possibly thank Jamaica Ross enough for agreeing to share her personal classroom design journey with all of us. Jamaica's willingness to be comfortable with the uncomfortable, to lead from behind, and to put adult privilege on hold has allowed her to co-create classroom environments with her students that nurture inclusivity, creativity, and opportunity. She is an inspiration!

Team Visual Artistry

I'd like to thank Angela Dyborn, Logan Williams, and the incredible Phoebe Solomon for sharing their photography and videography skills on this project. Thank you for honoring and beautifully capturing the incredible learning cultures and styles of each classroom space.

Team Cotsen

For each opportunity to discuss literacy and classroom design, thank you to the incredible lead team at the Cotsen Foundation for the Art of Teaching: Angela Bae, Lyndon Catayong, Vivian Galanti, Dianne Glinos, Barbara Golding, Tyler Sanders, and Jerry Harris.

Team Heinemann

For attending to each and every detail of this book with enthusiasm, precision, compassion, and care, thank you to my tremendously talented, patient, and positive team: Patty Adams, Steve Bernier, Cindy Black, Kimberly Capriola, Susan Cossaboom, Sarah Fournier, Michael Grover, Suzanne Heiser, Kalli Kirkpatrick, Krysten Lebel, Nadra Ostrom, Roderick Spelman, Paul Tomasyan, Elizabeth Tripp, and Lynette Winegarner. What a dream team!

I'd like to especially thank my editor, Holly Kim Price, who coached and cheered me on through a variety of personal "time-outs" and delay of games on this project. To see all of the pieces finally come together and actually become a book is incredible. Thank you for all of your guidance through each and every chapter (across three time zones, no less). Thank you, too, for all of your feedback and words of encouragement when I'd get stuck and struggle to say things clearly. This has been an amazing experience. What a gift you are to a first-time author!

My Home Team

A huge thanks to my extended family and friends. You all have consistently and faithfully cheered and supported me in every way imaginable, including and most especially each time we gather together.

A heartfelt thank-you to my parents, who have always been my number one support system and who first introduced me to the game of basketball. You knew when to stop the game and offer much-needed advice, support, and strategies. You also knew when to just let me play.

Thank you to my children: Tylia, Nathan, Jada, and Nico. It has been a unique experience to watch how each of you have intuitively figured out how to create spaces of your own. Whether under blankets and beds, beneath trees, or inside of forts, castles, tents, and collapsible tunnels, nothing seems to keep any of you from carving out space to breathe and play. I wish this for each of you, always.

Thank you to my partner and most favorite human being on this planet, Jonathan. There are no words to express how grateful I feel for your unending support of me and my work in so many big and small ways since the day we met. You inspire me to always be better and do better. Thank you for, well, everything.

Team Educators

Finally, to my fourth-grade teacher, Maria Nordquist, who first inspired my love of reading and wonder, and the reason why I decided to become a teacher. I want to also express my sincerest thanks to all of the educators who spend part of their precious dream life working through how to make classroom spaces feel more welcoming and just flat-out work better. Many of you, despite all of the demands on your time and energy, find time to ensure that your teaching philosophy, pedagogy, and classroom environment work together to create a positive learning experience for learners. I hope that you find some of the ideas, tips, and images of classrooms, from teachers just like you, to be insightful. I also hope you feel motivated to have more conversations with your students, colleagues, parents, and administrators about strategic classroom design. Tweet at me if you think I may be able to offer some additional support in this area @growingjessica. Go team!

Space Matters

Most days Jayvon's morning drop-off routine runs like clockwork. He skips along a path to his classroom, hangs up his backpack on one of the outdoor hooks, and removes his water bottle before nestling it into an empty cubby that is marked by an image from nature. Today, he chooses an acorn.

Jayvon then bounds out to the play yard to find a friend and await the morning bell with classmates. He is excited on the days he arrives to school a little bit early because he has time to join a friend or classmates climbing, swinging, or jumping atop the play apparatus. On other school mornings, Jayvon lingers near his backpack, waits until his mom kisses him goodbye on the cheek, and walks completely out of sight before taking out a treasure that he has secretly stored in a pocket. A fidget spinner, orange peels, Lego people, rocks, cars, and wood chips are among his favorites. Some treasures make it back home; many find a new home in the teacher's desk.

The morning bell rings. Jayvon and his classmates line up near other classes on the yard and begin a short walk to the entrance of their classroom while chatting about adventures or singing a favorite song. Before entering the classroom, he and his classmates greet their teacher at the door with a firm handshake and by making eye contact. After the teacher greeting, most mornings begin with independent reading followed by a welcome circle in the large open rug space. Jayvon's teacher gathers the children close to talk with them about the plan for the day and share any news, reminders, and announcements they might need to consider about the day or upcoming week. She also takes the opportunity to highlight kind and positive classroom behaviors she has been noticing and how those contribute to the feeling of safety and belonging for everyone. Next, it's time to sing a few favorite songs together. Everyone stands up and stretches before singing songs and chanting verses. The call-and-response and rhyming melodies that have gestures and movement are Jayvon's favorites. He tries hard to stay in his bubble of space while singing, which is hard at times because he loves to bounce, sway, wiggle, and move as he follows along with the rhythm.

As the music ends, storytelling begins. Jayvon walks over to a nearby shelf to pick up a piece of modeling clay from inside a small covered container. He quickly rejoins the group on the rug but sits on the perimeter now. He falls to his knees while gently kneading the clay with both thumbs and forefingers. His teacher turns on an electric candle near her chair, asks a student to dim the overhead lighting, and continues the read-aloud text that she began to read earlier in the week. Many of Jayvon's peers sit and listen to the story in partnerships or trios, some sit on pillows, others sit in chairs, and three students stand toward the back of the meeting area. Occasionally, Jayvon's teacher will guide the students to process what is happening in the text with a nearby thinking partner.

When the read-aloud ends, Jayvon jumps up and returns his piece of thinking clay, now an animal of some sort, to a nearby container on the shelf. He is eager to listen to the plan for the day and to begin the day's work at various project stations around the classroom. The projects on this day include a problem-solving investigation, exploring images and artifacts, caterpillar and butterfly habitat observations, learning a new vocabulary game, and art experiences with mixed media. As each group works independently, some students may receive additional support while in their group or be pulled out of the group for part of the time by the teacher to work in a targeted skill group. Students are invited to turn to a partner and share out a smooth exit and start-up routine for how they plan to move from the whole-group meeting area, quickly gather supplies, and get started at their project station. Once everyone briefly shares a game plan, Jayvon's teacher gives a nonverbal signal to leave the meeting area and begin their task.

Jayvon initiates his plan by carefully standing up and turning his body toward a work area adjacent to the whole-group space. He maneuvers his way around a few chatty peers, grabs a pen from a nearby supply caddy, and is first to find a seat at the lowered (table legs were removed) round table that displays a caterpillar habitat. As another group member passes out butterfly books, student sketchbooks, and magnifying glasses, Jayvon is excited to chat with a peer about how the caterpillars are suspending themselves on leaves and chewing away on host plants. Next a group member flips over a sand timer and they begin to discuss observations before recording their thinking in science sketchbooks. Before the work time ends, each budding entomologist takes a turn at sharing out with the group any unique observations that were made and documented into sketchbooks. The group responds to one another with a few connections, some predictions, and even more questions they have about caterpillars and butterflies.

A chime soon rings out and signals to everyone that it is time to clean up and rotate to another group. Jayvon and his classmates quickly finish sharing and collect books, sort observation tools, stack sketchbooks, and return all items to labeled baskets onto the science shelf nearby. When a second chime rings, Jayvon and his team head off to the next learning station, where they have opportunities to represent science topics and ideas through art.

How You Design Your Classroom Matters

As you follow Jayvon through a typical morning at school, you might be surprised by his level of independence or the limited amount of management from his teacher. What is not visible but very present in every moment of Jayvon's classroom learning experiences are the decisions Jayvon's teacher has made about classroom design. His environment is designed with a keen eye toward the type of learning tasks that can happen in flexible learning spaces. This includes lots of space to move, plenty of light, furniture options, and a variety of possible seating configurations, easy access to tools and supplies, and technology that is used to encourage thinking, innovation, and collaboration.

Only a small part of designing a learning space is about beautification and aesthetics. Reimagining a strategic learning space is mostly about being mindful of the evolving needs of learners. An emphasis is placed on safety and belonging so that learners are free to share, create, reflect, and collaborate in a whole group, in small groups, or on their own without fear of rejection or judgment. Additionally, designing a classroom environment means educators invite students to co-design structures and processes so that all stakeholders not just survive, but thrive across the school year.

Your Classroom Design Ignites Engagement

Notice how Jayvon's classroom teacher has set students up for success from the moment they arrive to school. Her drop-off system allows students to independently sort and store their own belongings. Once backpacks and jackets are put away and students are signed in, they can make decisions about how to spend time before the school day officially begins. In addition, her classroom activities are designed to happen in spaces that help ease the transition from home to school. Some students head out to the play yard; others read books, visit the discovery table, or play a card game in the classroom with a lingering parent or caregiver; and the remaining few

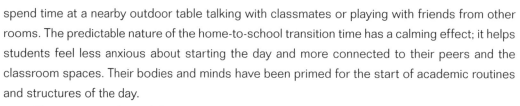

spend time at a nearby outdoor table talking with classmates or playing with friends from other rooms. The predictable nature of the home-to-school transition time has a calming effect; it helps students feel less anxious about starting the day and more connected to their peers and the classroom spaces. Their bodies and minds have been primed for the start of academic routines and structures of the day.

The activities planned for Jayvon and his classmates also intend to promote curiosity. Drawing on a study by Gruber, Gelman, and Ranganath (2014), Marianne Stenger (2014) wrote, "curiosity puts the brain in a state that allows it to learn and retain any kind of information, like a vortex that sucks in what you are motivated to learn, and also everything around it. So, if a teacher is able to arouse students' curiosity about something they're naturally motivated to learn, they'll be better prepared to learn things that they would normally consider boring or difficult." Jayvon and his classmates are challenged with lots of decision work that builds curiosity and leads to engagement and ownership of their learning. Where should they sit? Where will they get the materials they need? How should they start? Students in Jayvon's classroom are encouraged to work as a team and utilize the classroom space to prep for learning opportunities and seek answers and solutions. For example, a small group of students might begin a task in a designated part of the room using an inquiry approach. They might make observations, ask questions about the realia on the table or on their devices, and then collect and pass out materials needed for learning, determine seating arrangement, work together, share findings with one another, and of course, clean up. By design and with support from their teacher, students are encouraged to learn because they're given responsibilities and a space to think, make a plan, and work together. Engagement is ignited when students feel ownership of their classroom environment and play a role in making decisions about how the teaching and learning will occur.

The opportunity to engage and collaborate alongside peers in well-imagined classroom spaces is also a chance to learn important skills about boundaries and behaviors. For many, learning alongside peers, rather than going it alone, is in and of itself engaging. In each of the different classroom spaces, whole-group rug area, library area, and small-group and individualized learning stations, students learn from one another about acceptable and expected behaviors and how to negotiate disagreements. Fostering respect with how each classmate makes their own contributions to the group without fear of judgment or rejection allows each member to participate more fully in a learning task, decreases misbehaviors, and increases engagement.

Your Classroom Design Helps Students Stay on Task

Once Jayvon's teacher greets all students by name, makes eye contact, and shakes hands with each of them, they reunite as a classroom community in a large open space at the center of their classroom for songs, stories, and brief announcements. Students know to start the day by first meeting in the larger communal space, forming a welcome circle for greetings and songs, and performing a movement activity. A little while later they reconfigure the seating arrangement for a story, class news, and school updates before going off to work in individualized or smaller, more intimate group configurations around the classroom. In the whole-group space, the expectation is to participate in ways that honor contributions made by the classroom community. Class norms in whole-group settings might include raising hands to signal a desire to share an idea or add on to someone else's thinking (until students are ready to participate without raising hands); using a talking stick to direct focus and attention to the speaker; using timing devices like schedules, sand timers, and chimes to remind group members to practice attentive listening while waiting to respond; and creating a seating chart with assigned spaces until these tools are no longer needed. In small-group spaces, the expectation is to collaborate with one another to accomplish a learning task or goal. Class norms in a small-group setting include taking turns, making plans, collecting materials, speaking calmly with one another, using an appropriate indoor volume, respecting ideas that might be different than their own, and cleaning up by sorting, returning, and organizing materials to nearby storage areas and shelves.

Establishing norms and co-authoring routines and protocols that correspond to specific spaces or areas in the classroom are examples of how a teacher might strategically use the classroom environment to help students stay on task. With practice, students better understand how their environment works and are able anticipate and navigate respectful and welcoming behaviors in the various learning areas around the classroom more successfully (Rohrer and Samson 2014). For example, as students become more familiar with the classroom library routines of book selection, book care, and the kinds of learning opportunities that can happen there, engagement levels will likely increase along with the ability to stay on task.

In addition to keeping in mind the emotional and behavioral relationships between the learner and the physical learning environment, it is important to think about the cognitive work that the learner is engaged in and how this work also promotes on-task behaviors in the learning space. Lessons that are intentionally planned with students in mind will optimize student learning goals. Educators like Jayvon's teacher and her grade-level colleagues often meet together to plan curriculum using standards, assessment data, and a variety of resources. They plan with an eye toward novelty and sustaining curiosity, as well as using provocations to spark new ideas and questions.

Learning experiences that are planned with intention and enhanced by the layout of the physical classroom space assist students with staying on task. In their book *Classroom Instruction That Works: Research-Based Strategies for Increasing Student Achievement*, authors Marzano, Pickering, and Pollock noted that "no instructional strategy works equally well in all situations" (2001, 8). Simply using and teaching the strategies as prescribed in a teacher's guide, for example, does not raise student achievement; teachers must also understand how, when, where, and why to use them.

Classroom spaces support students in a variety of ways so they can remain focused on their learning with minimal distractions. With intentional planning these strategically designed areas can help foster social, emotional, behavioral, and cognitive growth and well-being for all learners.

Your Classroom Design Cultivates Collaboration

Jayvon's teacher, like so many of us, works hard to nurture home and school relationships because she knows they matter most. Providing space for students to collaborate with peers, teachers, teaching assistants, and parent volunteers requires thinking about how best to utilize our small classroom spaces in big ways. At the ground level, teachers understand that for students to successfully collaborate with one another and adults, the classroom environment must feel open enough for students to easily communicate feelings, thoughts, and actions. To collaborate well, students typically need spaces they can think and work in both individually and collectively. They need a physical environment that promotes safe and positive social learning opportunities through innovation, tinkering, problem-solving, and reflecting with one another.

However, classroom spaces are not created equal. The average classroom is approximately 750 square feet (25 × 30). Go ahead and set aside 150 square feet for teacher space, typically at the front or back of the classroom. Then set aside the 25 square feet (5 × 5) of often unusable space near the doors and/or window emergency exit. Finally, divide the remaining space by the average number of students (25) in a room. The result is about 23 square feet per student, which is arguably not a lot of space in which to work (Abramson 2015).

To think about what it would take to design a space that promotes collaboration, teachers must know their students, consider age-appropriate tasks, and envision the space for its opportunities rather than its challenges. Spaces large enough to fit the entire class might lend themselves to beautiful communal experiences where students are engaged in deep discussions, song, literature, fascinating content-area topics, laughing, taking on challenges, and brainstorming solutions together collaboratively. The experiences that happen in these larger spaces propel students forward as a collective.

Classroom spaces designed for smaller groups or individuals allow students to have more personalized learning experiences. Chairs or pillows surrounding a small table or a standing table pushed up against a back wall might feel more comfortable and intimate for some learners. Some students might take more ownership over their learning when collaboration occurs in small groups or when they have the chance to first work on something on their own before sharing out ideas with a partner.

All of the areas in your classroom, no matter how big or small, can be utilized in strategic ways. Spending time thinking about how to optimize a whole-group space for the classroom community and how to use all of the smaller, surrounding spaces can cultivate endless and exciting opportunities for inclusive collaboration.

Your Classroom Design Supports Student Achievement

Jayvon's classmates regularly come together to greet each other and negotiate tasks in the whole-group meeting area. As the year progresses, each classmate can begin to anticipate activities held here and acceptable ways to participate in them. This community meeting space not only becomes a place to practice welcome rituals and have powerful discussions, it becomes a whole-class teaching and learning hub where students can press on other each other's ideas. It is often a teacher's favorite time of day to gather together, offer feedback, provide clarity, and alleviate confusion around classroom behaviors that impact student performance. Time spent together, reflecting on behaviors and classroom expectations, discussing self-management and self-regulation strategies, or having fun role-playing participation scenarios with one another is important for the growth of all students. For those students who sometimes have trouble taking risks or struggle with some of the behavioral norms of a traditional school setting, this time is both grounding and practical as it supports how they interact (perform) in daily activities.

British researchers, led by Professor Peter Barrett, collected data and concluded, "Classroom design could be attributed to a 25% impact, positive or negative, on a student's progress over the course of an academic year. The difference between the best and worst designed classrooms covered in the study? A full year's worth of academic progress" (Barrett et al. 2015). The study also measured design elements that included lighting, noise levels, air quality, furniture layout, flexibility, and storage availability.

We can build opportunities for all students to experience academic success without shame or blame through the way we design lessons and projects, the variety of spaces we offer, and the kind of access we provide to materials. Many educators agree that what drives the learning space configuration is the type of task, number of students involved in the project, and each student's role. Ideally, students have multiple opportunities across the day to support their own achievement by making choices about where to work in the room, how to go about tasks, and whether to work individually or collaborate with one another.

Students who struggle with social norms often affect teacher expectations, which impact student performance. Psychologists Robert Rosenthal and Lenore Jacobson "found that expectations affect teachers' moment-to-moment interactions with the children they teach in a thousand almost invisible ways. Teachers give the students that they expect to succeed more time to answer questions, more specific feedback, and more approval: They consistently touch, nod and smile at those kids more" (Rosenthal and Jacobson 2003). In his classroom, Jayvon knows that if he gets a wiggly or bouncy feeling during storytelling time, it's not a bad feeling. He has been taught to use the strategy of taking a standing position near the side or back of the meeting area to help him listen better, learn better, and participate in classroom conversations with confidence and competence. His access to curriculum has not been decreased or taken away by being sent to the time-out chair or to "visit" another classroom for a short break. Jayvon has learned that if his hands start to have that busy "buzzy" feeling, rather than swing his arms around and accidently touch others, he can squeeze or shake them out. He can also collect a piece of modeling clay provided by his teacher and use that fidgety hand energy to knead or sculpt. Each of these options allows Jayvon to remain in the lesson, stay connected to the group, and continue learning.

From My Experience

Along with ten years of moving cabinets, desks, chairs, and tables back and forth across my own classroom floors, this book comes from my own personal experiences with helping hundreds of kindergarten–middle school classroom teachers across the country rethink their learning environments—either during summer professional development workshops or impromptu classroom makeover sessions.

I taught at Corinne A. Seeds University Elementary School (currently known as the UCLA Lab School). It was while working here as a demonstration teacher that I learned the most about classroom design and its impact on teaching and learning. A few aha moments included (no surprise here) the importance of light and natural elements to create a sense of calm, relieve stress, and improve cognitive function (Kaplan and Kaplan 1989; Tanner 2009; Wells 2000) in the classroom. I became a bargain shopper for indoor plants at local nurseries and swap meets, and a bit of a green thumb, usually picking up something for my own apartment space as well.

I also learned about color and its influence on emotion, student behavior, and performance. I began to think about and experiment with color palettes on my walls, display boards, and even with furniture. I stopped decorating my bulletin boards with brightly colored butcher paper and matching borders. Instead I learned to use muted colors to prevent overstimulation.

The idea of flexible seating configurations was not a new revelation, but at the lab school I learned to take flexible to the next level. Colleagues inspired me to make clipboards readily available and to raise, lower, and remove the adjustable legs of a table to create different kinds of seating or standing options for students. Who knew this would be one of the easiest (and cheapest) ways to impact student learning? My students seemed more engaged in their tasks when they were given options. Would they work alone, with a partner, or in small groups? Would they work standing up, sitting, kneeling, leaning, or lying on the floor?

I continued to explore classroom design when I became a staff developer. In addition to supporting teachers with literacy and math, I had ongoing conversations about the impact classroom design had on teaching and learning. With the help of colleagues and educators, I learned to consider the implications of one design over another—what it means to move in the space, how to think about furniture as a tool for student learning, how to teach students about classroom layout, and how to create an environment that is conducive to learning for both teachers and students. Ultimately, I learned to help teachers think more strategically about classroom design.

What You'll Find in This Book

This book is designed for educators interested in learning more about the factors that contribute to well-designed classroom spaces that connect with students and help teachers more effectively navigate the world of teaching and learning. Each chapter is full of photographs of classrooms ranging from grades K to 8. I share predictable challenges, one or two transcribed sample lessons, a chart with specific lesson suggestions, and answers to some common questions in an "If–Then" section.

You can read this book from cover to cover or jump into a section that resonates with you; perhaps it connects to a challenge or opportunity in your classroom, everything from How can I create a learning space where everyone feels welcome and a sense of belonging? to What do I do about the daily traffic jam that occurs at the supply station? to How long should it take for my students to transition into the classroom from recess? We get used to constantly juggling what is in and out of our control. Sometimes we start off the school year without certain supplies, the arrival of new students with only a moment's notice, and broken classroom furniture, but we make it work. I am confident that you'll find the information, makeover stories, and photographs from educators—just like you—helpful and inspiring. You, too, have permission to be creative and resourceful in your practice, going beyond the surface-level work of simply creating aesthetically-pleasing learning spaces. Attention to classroom layout and co-authoring with students about each space's rituals and routines will inspire a greater sense of belonging as well as provide students with opportunities to be part of an engaged, focused, and collaborative community of learners.

Chapter 1

What do we mean by classroom design? In this chapter we'll explore the basic layout of your space from the ground up. We'll consider how to make room for a whole-group space, small-group spaces, individual work spaces, and your teacher space. When you are reimagining your classroom, it can feel overwhelming, so I'll show you how to start with a simple layout plan.

Chapter 2

How can we set up our classrooms in strategic ways to cultivate curiosity, belonging, and academic growth? In this chapter, we'll explore the other classroom work spaces—the library, multimedia learning space, makerspace, play area, content area, and art space—and think about how they can be designed to help breathe life and inspiration into your learning journey with students.

Chapter 3

How can we help students move, transition, and interact with one another and the classroom environment in ways that feel conscious and connected? We'll highlight the most commonly congested traffic areas and challenges. In addition, we'll consider ways to help students transition with more intention and purpose and how to co-author plans with your students to efficiently gather supplies and complete assigned tasks and projects.

Chapter 4

Which elements of design make the most impact on teaching and learning according to research, and which are the most budget friendly? We'll take a closer look at what the research says about the effects of light, color, sound, and natural elements on the classroom environment. Then we'll explore practical ways to incorporate these design elements into your own classroom.

Chapter 5

Follow one teacher's journey as she strategically designs her classroom space. See before-and-after images and learn about the ups and downs she encounters along the way.

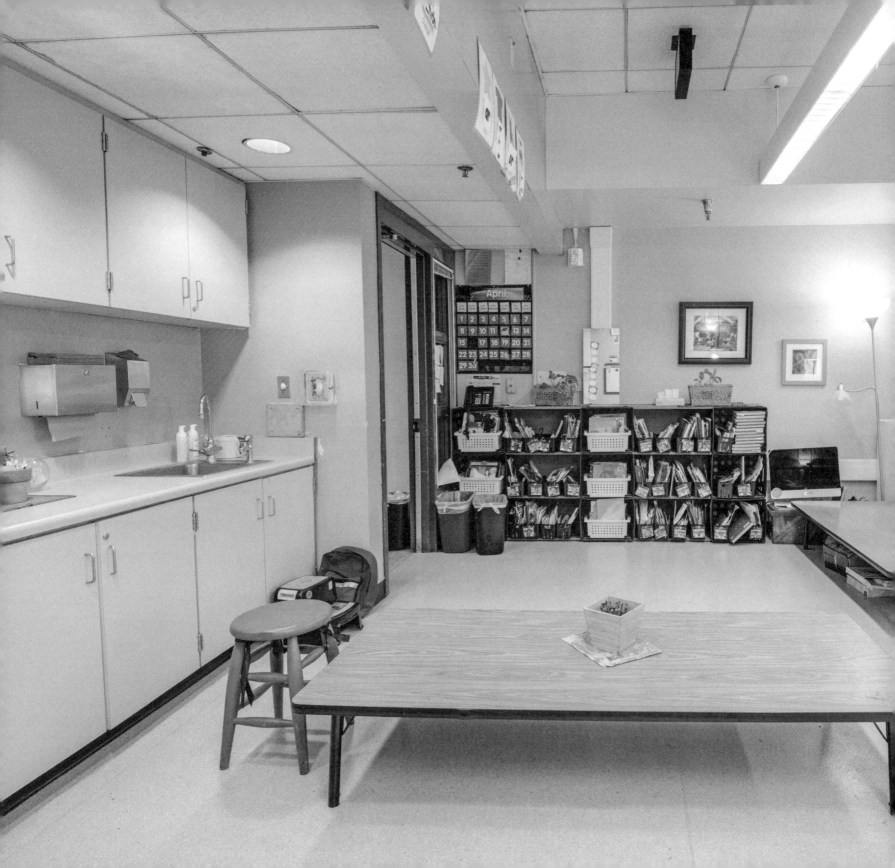

1

Creating a Physical Environment That Empowers Learners

Jamaica, an eighteen-year veteran teacher from Long Beach, California, was ready to start the school year at a new school. After teaching fifth grade the year before, she was looking forward to teaching third grade again. In last year's fifth-grade classroom, she started to think about classroom design with her students. Together, they made changes based on everyone's ideas and feedback. Jamaica wanted to continue her journey with strategic classroom design in her new school setting with her new third-grade students. (You'll see photos from Jamaica's third- and fifth-grade classrooms in this book!)

One August morning, just seven days before the first day of school, we agreed to meet in her new classroom to talk about the physical environment. She was intrigued by the opportunity to strategically design a classroom space from the ground up. Her new school was in the process of being renovated so she and her colleagues were asked to set up shop in temporary portable class-rooms for the upcoming school year. We began by walking around the classroom space. Her classroom had no tables, desks, chairs, shelving, or cabinets; they were to be delivered later that week. We stood near her whiteboard and talked about goals she had for her learners this year and ideas she had about teaching in her new classroom space. She wanted to create a place where students felt safe and seen. She envisioned a space large enough for everyone to meet as a community throughout the day, and some small-group work spaces where she could work with

> *The real voyage of discovery consists not in seeking new landscapes, but in having new eyes.*
>
> —MARCEL PROUST,
> *IN SEARCH OF LOST TIME*

1

just a few learners at a time. One of her personal goals this year was to also make sure students maximized their learning time. All of her ideas seemed like wonderful starting points.

Teachers spend a lot of time inside their classrooms. We often arrive early in the morning to prepare for our students and to catch up on administrative duties; we stay late into the afternoon to help kids with homework, meet with parents and grade-level team members, and to clean and organize our classrooms. According to Jim Hull and Mandy Newport's 2011 article "Time in School: How Does the U.S. Compare?" for the Center for Public Education, conservative estimates say US students spend on average 11,700 hours of their lives in our classrooms during their K–12 school experience (quoted in Cheryan et al. 2014). With that many hours spent with students inside of classroom walls, it makes sense for us to be mindful, even strategic, when we plan out a space.

Space matters. It matters because the places we inhabit play a key role in how we think, feel, and react to things. It matters because when we are uncomfortable in a space, it affects our ability to learn. Space can have both a positive and a negative impact on our decision-making process. Each time we design a new layout plan for our classroom, we influence the way our students learn, participate, collaborate, and grow. Keeping our students and their needs at the forefront of strategic classroom design is what makes it strategic. Will our classroom design promote and encourage more positive learning outcomes, or will it deprive and discourage learners from using their voice, taking risks, and owning their learning?

Whether you are a new teacher designing your classroom for the first time or a veteran teacher ready to consider a small change or complete makeover, start by reimagining your physical layout or floor plan. Be sure to include different-sized spaces for students to join together and collaborate.

Develop a Floor Plan

What do you notice that is unique about your current space? Is there space for all of your learners to gather as a whole group? In small groups away from their seats? Individually and away from others? One way to begin this exciting journey into strategic classroom design is to imagine or reimagine all space configurations by drawing it out on paper or a whiteboard, or creating a digital sketch of the space, imagining it first as a blank slate or canvas where anything is possible. See Figure 1.1 for an example of how Jamaica used graph paper to capture proportion and the dimensions of the layout in her new classroom space.

Begin by sketching out the perimeters, making sure to consider the space around doors, whiteboards, display boards, and windows in your classroom. You'll want to make sure there is ample room for students to enter and exit the classroom. You will also think carefully about corners. You'll want to keep corners clear on your floor plan sketch as they are prime real estate "nooks" for learning. Corners tend to be quieter and feel less busy. Figure 1.2 shows how Jamaica reserved corner space as well as space around the door, boards, and windows.

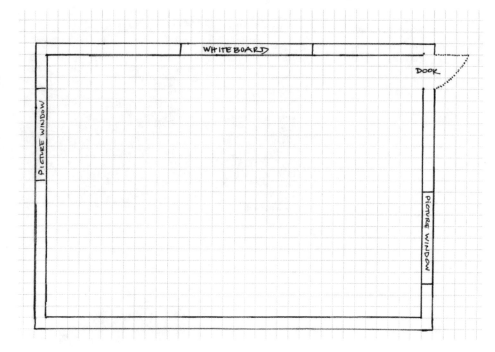

Figure 1.1 Consider using graph paper to sketch out the space dimensions of your classroom.

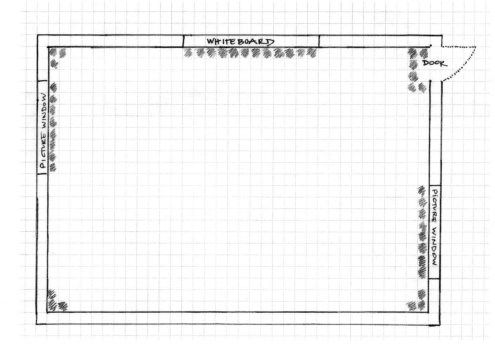

Figure 1.2 Jamaica shaded in areas on her layout grid to preserve space near the door, whiteboard, corners, and windows.

3

Figure 1.3 Middle school classroom. Rather than a large area rug, Julia preferred smaller rugs that give students more space when gathering together as a whole class. Small rugs are also easier to wash and care for.

Figure 1.4 Middle school classroom. Learners gathered into a central space using an amphitheater-style configuration. Tiered seating provided Aimee's students with a few different seating options. Seating options support positive participation goals (students feel more comfortable and able to focus) during whole-group lessons and partnership discussions.

Figure 1.5 Fifth-grade classroom. Instead of placing the large-group meeting area in a corner of the room, Jamaica experimented with centralizing it and framing the space with an area rug that offered students options to sit on the floor or use chairs, crates, stools, and cushions.

Figure 1.6 First-grade classroom. Shayla created a larger open space by design so that her primary students could move, collaborate, and meet in different learning configurations using the same space across the day.

Figure 1.7 Kindergarten classroom. Creating a large-group space in a smaller than normal classroom presents a challenge. Rosanne's decision to use multifunctional furnishings kept the area feeling light, airy, and open.

Whole-Group Meeting Area

Since it's the largest space consideration, tackle your whole-group space first. Ideally, the meeting area holds everyone comfortably. It allows the whole class to join together for lessons, discussions, and activities before students head off to work independently or in small groups (see Figures 1.3–1.7). There are many benefits to carving out as large of a whole-group space as you can, no matter which grade level you teach. Where else will your community meet to have conversations, share news, tell tales, explore ideas, and push one another's thinking?

Having students come together in close proximity for short periods of time provides invaluable whole-group learning experiences. The whole-group space also gives the teacher additional opportunities to informally assess and differentiate instruction for students. For example, it allows the teacher to coach into participation behaviors in the moment and to redirect, prompt, or positively reinforce as needed. A meeting area also provides students with multiple opportunities to turn and process their thinking with a partner. Proximity helps students become more accountable to each other and gives the teacher additional opportunities to listen to partnership thinking, support individual learning goals, and support language development through coaching, prompting, or demonstrating in the moment. Of course, whole-class teaching and differentiated instruction can

Furniture Considerations: To Rug or Not to Rug

Some teachers have strong feelings about area rugs in the classroom. For some educators it's a nonissue; rugs are a part of the school culture. In the primary grades, almost every teacher is expected to have one in their classroom. Primary students traditionally gather on or around the area rug for minilessons, class meetings, interactive read-aloud lessons, discussions, and debates. Some upper-elementary and middle school teachers also embrace the idea of a meeting space that includes a rug or some form of carpeting. For other educators, rugs are an eyesore or can present a health concern without proper cleaning and maintenance across the school year. The rug itself is not as important as carving out a space or a way for students to gather together as a community of learners.

be accomplished without a central meeting area, but it may feel more challenging to get around to everyone quickly since students are spread out or seated behind desks. Gathering briefly as a class in a designated meeting space is similar to a team coming together. Imagine it's the fourth quarter of a big game and your coach calls a time-out. The clock stops. Your team gathers near the bench area for a huddle. The closeness of the huddle contains the energy and urgency of the moment. It allows the coach to make eye contact with players and share words of inspiration. It's at this moment, much like when we gather for a minilesson, that the team becomes one.

Whole-group meeting space design will typically match the grade level you teach. Meeting spaces in primary classrooms will look different from those in upper-elementary, middle, and high school. With older students, you'll want to create a space that has some flexibility and can grow with the students. Give preteen and young adolescent learners options to stand, kneel, or lean during the lesson. You might also create a tiered or amphitheater-style seating arrangement where students are given the choice to choose from a variety of seating options—on the floor, in chairs, atop of stools, and even standing at the back or on the sidelines.

As you start to think about where to place your meeting area, consider the accessibility of the space from anywhere in the room and imagine the traffic patterns that can be built around it. The more open, accessible, and flexible the space, the greater the opportunity for thinking and learning to occur.

Figure 1.8 shows how Jamaica began to envision her classroom space. We cut colored sticky notes to represent the planned spaces in her classroom and tried to size them to scale. Move sticky notes around until you find a configuration that feels like it might work for your students (the true test is when your learners arrive). When considering your whole-group space, ask yourself these questions:

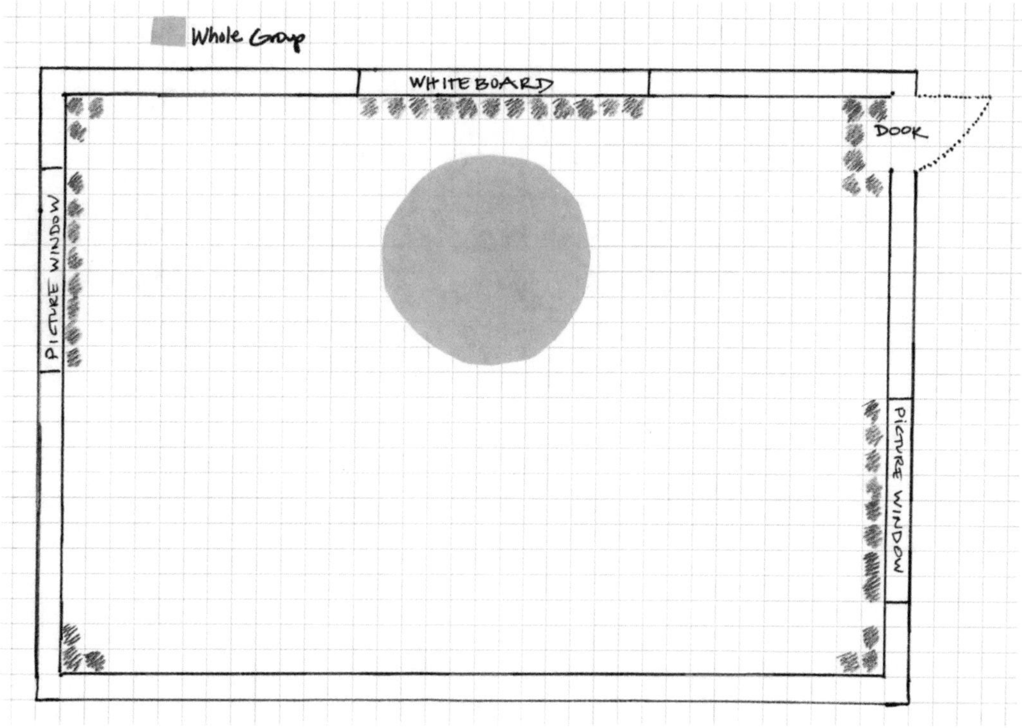

Figure 1.8 Jamaica cut up a green sticky note to imagine where her meeting/rug areas might go. Green = meeting/rug areas

7

- Is there enough space for everyone to sit comfortably?

- Where are the multiple access points to enter and exit the space?

- Are there any blind spots or obstructed views of the whiteboard in the central teaching area?

- Is there access within the central teaching area for learners to present or demonstrate learning?

Once you've allocated space on your floor plan for the whole-class meeting area, consider taping it out on your actual floor, or visiting a classroom design website like https://floorplanner.com or https://www.smartdraw.com to input the dimensions and/or create a virtual classroom layout design. Remember to always take into account the age, size, and number of students as well as any learning or ambulatory needs.

Furniture Considerations: Seating

Many educators choose to furnish the classroom meeting area with <u>flexible seating options</u> for students and for themselves. Many teachers now use technology as they teach and prefer to sit on stools, in rocking chairs, or in ergonomic chairs that offer back support. Seating options can be noisy. Consider muffling furniture noises so that the dragging and pushing of chairs doesn't disrupt teaching and learning. Some teachers collect used tennis balls or use rounded pieces of felt or self-stick furniture pads on the legs of chairs.

Small-Group Work Spaces

Small-group work spaces are places within the classroom where students can go to work on assignments or projects in collaboration with or seated near peers (see Figures 1.9–1.14). Teachers also use small-group spaces to meet with students and to differentiate instruction after whole-group teaching experiences in the meeting area. Small-group work spaces give students the opportunity to

- revisit learning concepts with differentiated skill and strategy support;

- help learners develop effective communication and collaboration skills; and

- help learners develop and practice their interpersonal skills.

It's not just about coming together in small groups; it's about creating space that fosters more equitable opportunities for learning.

As you think about what kinds of learning opportunities your students will need, let's return to your floor plan. Now that you have an idea about the location of your whole-class meeting space, think next about configuring small-group work spaces. Consider how many tabletop or desktop surfaces you have. Since you'll most likely have students concurrently working on electronic tablets and clipboards (which don't require a dedicated space), you can finally let go of the conventional wisdom that dictates one desk and one chair for every student, and begin to embrace new, more fluid classroom designs that give learners more work surface options.

Be sure to also take advantage of even the smallest spaces. Where are your nooks, niches, and alcoves? Young learners are extremely savvy when it comes to transforming odd, awkward, and smallish classroom spaces into ideal workplaces. As long as it is safe, give learners the option to work under tables, in tight corners, near or just outside of doors and hallways. If given the chance, students will typically make the most out of any area in the classroom.

It's not always possible to make your own decisions about classroom furniture. Usually you make do with what's already in the classroom or nearby in your school's storage overflow area. Since you're thinking about getting more creative with your space and furniture, be sure to read and ask about your school policy and procedures. Check out local organizations like the one in Los Angeles called Two Bit Circus Foundation (twobitcircus.org), formerly known as Trash for Teaching (T4T.org). The foundation cultivates partnerships with local organizations to recycle their unused and unwanted materials. It's a gold mine for educators trying to enhance their STEAM (Science, Technology, Engineering, Arts, and Mathematics) curriculum and create a makerspace or design lab. You can purchase a membership or apply to be a grant recipient. Another nonprofit organization that connects businesses and folks who want to donate directly to teachers and classrooms is donorschoose.org. This organization supports educators

Figure 1.9 Kindergarten classroom. Rosanne's classroom design allowed her young learners to move seamlessly from the whole-class meeting area into collaborative pods. Notice the variety of work surfaces and flexible seating choices that promote collaboration and discussion (Brooks 2011).

Figure 1.10 First-grade classroom. Shayla's classroom layout provided a variety of work surfaces at adjustable heights. Learners could work while sitting or kneeling at tables, stretching out on the floor with a clipboard, laptop, or tablet, or even perching themselves near a bright window overlooking the playground for inspiration.

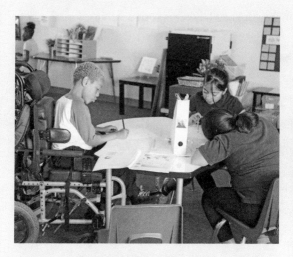

Figure 1.11 Third-grade classroom. Jamaica created lots of space and opportunity for students to make choices about where to sit and how to best use their space to work collaboratively or independently. Developing student choice and agency around seating cultivates a sense of pride and ownership of the classroom space.

Figure 1.12 Fourth-grade classroom. Lori met with a few of her mathematicians who found a spot on the carpet in the whole-group meeting area during independent work time.

Figure 1.13 Fourth-grade classroom. Lori's second-floor classroom had windows that let in plenty of natural light and a low storage unit that increased space efficiency. Not coincidentally, her students often met in small groups near the windows and used the storage unit as extra seating during book talks and in writing groups.

Figures 1.14a and 1.14b Middle school classroom. Substituting individual desks with round tables and purchasing a few stools at a local secondhand shop gave Julia's space a more modern and collaborative appeal, which helped learners feel more connected.

with the means to reinvent their classroom environment with flexible seating options, storage items, books, and technology.

If you're fortunate to have a classroom budget where you can make choices about supplies and furniture, be sure your selections are strategic. This may mean ordering your classroom supplies separately from the school-wide bulk order. Go ahead and try to be picky about your options:

- Choose tables or desks that have adjustable heights.
- Consider purchasing a variety of flexible seating options (balance balls, stools, or wobbly stools).
- Look into ergonomically designed furniture with armrests that support back and posture health.

Some students prefer to stand, so if it's possible, order height-adjustable tables or desks. If students like to sit on the floor, look for low-to-the-ground tables. Coffee tables also work really well. Are there any extra small shelving units or storage systems available, just floating around your school site? If so, place them near small-group work areas so students can access the materials they need quickly and easily. I know so many teachers who spend their own money to purchase furniture or storage systems. Resist the urge; the costs add up quickly. Start by taking inventory of what's readily available. Be sure to share your ideas and classroom design plans with colleagues in case they'd like to donate an item from their classroom that would be a good fit in yours.

Furniture Considerations: Desks Versus Tables

Rather than think about desks versus tables, think about how you can orient students in ways that allow them to more easily turn and face one another, make eye contact, and work efficiently on collaborative tasks and activities. You don't have to choose one or the other; why not have a combination? Whatever you decide, use Figure 1.15 to understand some of the pros and cons for either option.

Desk

Pros

Commonly found

Maximizes focus

Increases productivity

Height adjustable

When pushed together, could allow for more flexible groupings

Stores and organizes personal items

Cons

Sometimes bulky

Takes effort to reconfigure

Conceals items

Non-adjustable

Table

Pros

Takes up less space

Easier to move around

Facilitates collaboration and creative thinking

Height adjustable

Allows for more flexible seating options

Easier to keep clean

Cons

Size needs to match space

More talking

Less personal space

Less storage

Harder to separate students during assessments

Figure 1.15 Desks Versus Tables: Pros and Cons

It's also interesting to note the shape of your desks and tables. Researchers at the Barrow Neurological Institute share studies about how sharp corners appear brighter and harder to look at. Sharp edges interrupt thought. Rounded edges on desks and tables are easier for our eyes to process, according to Professor Jürg Nänni, authority on visual cognition. As young children, we are conditioned to stay away from sharp objects. Hard edges keep us on alert while smooth edges are more conducive to calm and comfort (Troncoso, Macknik, and Martinez-Conde 2005, 2009; Troncoso et al. 2007).

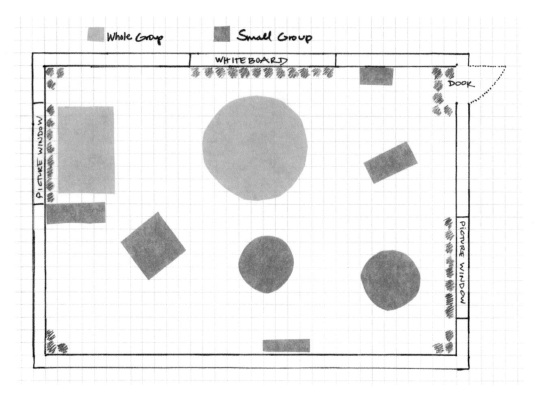

Figure 1.16 Jamaica added orange sticky notes to represent where her small-group meeting areas might go. Green = area rugs; orange = tabletop surfaces for small-group work spaces

Once you have designated the larger meeting areas, add in where you think small-group tables or desks for students might go. Figure 1.16 shows how Jamaica envisioned where her small-group areas might go. Don't forget that your whole-group meeting area can also be used as an impromptu small-group space when the class isn't gathered together.

Individual Work Spaces

We are all different. We have our own individual style and preferences for learning. Take a minute to reflect on yours. Where do you feel most productive? What do you need around you to help yourself focus? Think of what could happen if we strategically created classroom spaces that felt instantly welcoming and made it easier to focus on learning (see Figures 1.17–1.21).

Oftentimes before or after basketball practice in high school I was eager to have some additional court time to myself. I wanted to work on my moves or practice a drill that I had recently learned but was not able to get right. Generally, the drills and plays we learned during the season

Figure 1.17 Kindergarten classroom. After making their book selections in the classroom library area, emergent readers in Rosanne's classroom liked to spread out around the classroom using floor mats. Sometimes they could even be found under tables during independent reading time.

Figure 1.18 First-grade classroom. Writers in Shayla's classroom chose both a work space and a flexible seating option before settling into a task. Choices for seating options included chairs, balance balls, crates, and wobbly stools.

Figure 1.19 Fifth-grade classroom. Jamaica often met and conferred with students in the spaces they chose to work. She found that venturing out to where they had settled in and started working helped students better ease into conversations about their learning.

Figure 1.20 Third-grade classroom. Learners in Jamaica's classroom were expected to carve out their own private work spaces if working next to a partner proved challenging. Analy found a quiet spot along the perimeter of the classroom, added a few pillows, and used a clipboard as her writing surface.

Figure 1.21 Fifth-grade classroom. Individual nook and cranny spaces are gold mines for learners who prefer to feel hidden or work alone. Don't overlook these possible areas as viable work spaces. Notice the spaces for learning in between furniture, between storage cabinets, and under windows.

were taught as the whole team gathered around, listened, then scrimmaged each afternoon. I was and still am the kind of learner that just needed a bit more time to think through the plays, mentally understand my role and responsibilities, and physically walk through each step on my own a few times.

In many classrooms, there doesn't seem to be enough time, space, or resources for learners like me to work independently for a little while. Often we expect students to find their seat, get started on their assignment, and await further instructions. However, there are many students who would benefit and feel more confident in their work if they had a chance to spend some additional

Furniture Considerations: Variety and Flexibility

If we want students to feel empowered to make their own choices about what kind of independent work space may work best for them, then variety and flexibility matter.

1. Variety—Each of us have personal preferences when it comes to where we feel the most productive. Many of us find inspiration in a big comfy chair; for others it's sitting at a table in a library or coffee shop; and for some of us it's while walking, standing around, or shooting hoops. It all depends on the learner and the task. Gathering a variety of furniture options will take time. Start with what you have. Then pay attention to what's happening in your local community, like stoop sales, garage and yard sales, and secondhand stores. If you live near storage units or colleges, keep an eye out at the end of the school year for sidewalk sale freebies and discounts.

2. Flexibility—For an independent work area to feel like it's a good fit, it can help to think through how a learner might rearrange the furniture to make it more conducive to accomplishing a task or goal. I am constantly amazed to see students, when given the chance, completely own a space. Trusting learners to choose a space and make their own seating decisions gives us new insight into their creative processes.

time on their own working through ideas and solutions with targeted teacher feedback. We must remove the stigma attached to needing more time or working slowly through a task.

Before jumping head first into flexible seating options, establish routines and agreements that help your learning community feel unified. Once the classroom participation agreements are in place, you might start exploring alternative individual work spaces (see Figure 1.22). Allow students to select their own work space. Giving students the choice of work space is one way to develop agency and decision-making skills. Whether learners are sitting, standing, or lying spread out on the floor, on an area rug, or under a table, it's all about getting students to know what they need in order to nurture their own personal productivity.

Another way to ease students into flexible seating is to try it out during different parts of the day. Perhaps students start the day in their assigned seats and then later on in the day are offered choices about where they'd like to independently work and whether they'd prefer to stand, kneel, lean, or sit. Once learners understand how flexible seating works and how to be productive in their self-selected work spaces, you can expect it to become a classroom norm.

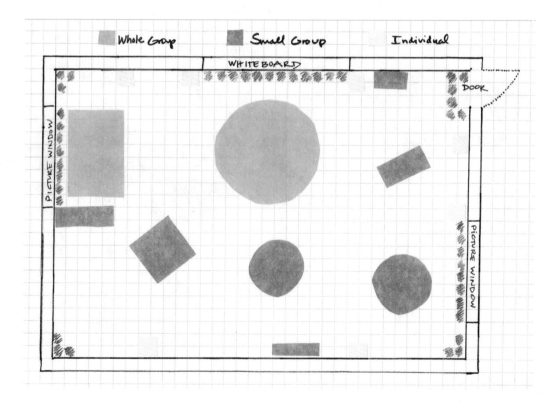

Figure 1.22 In addition to small-group work spaces, Jamaica added yellow sticky notes to represent individual work spaces. The whole-group meeting area and the small-group work areas are also options for independent work. Green = area rugs; orange = tabletop surfaces for small-group work spaces; yellow = individual work spaces

Teacher Work Spaces

But where will you be in all of this? You'll want to make sure you carve out a little space for yourself in the classroom. Consider two distinct areas—one that will be your main teaching location and the other that can serve as a storage hub for easy access to the resources you rely on most and need at your fingertips. When designing a teaching space, think about which teaching tools you will want to store nearby. Will you be using an overhead projector and screen, whiteboard,

▲ **Figure 1.23** Middle school classroom. Julia's workplace included an ergonomic chair with simple adjustment options and used two long tables and containers to manage the organizational demands of the classroom. The tables also served as a student supply station, a place to hold teaching materials, and a technology hub for her computer and document camera.

▶ **Figure 1.24** Middle school classroom. Aimee attempted to keep clutter at a distance by not using her desk as a storage space. Since she rarely used it during the day, students were invited to use it as their own independent work space.

▲ **Figure 1.25** Kindergarten classroom. Notice the shelving area behind Rosanne's workplace. This is where she stored curriculum manuals, resource files, lesson plans, and essential supplies like pens, pencils, staplers, and snacks. The table surface also doubled as a small-group work area where Rosanne could pull small groups and differentiate instruction.

mobile easel, chart paper, or all of the above? If so, then consider having a few baskets or containers or a shelving unit to house your pens, markers, books, and other supplies near your teaching space. There should be a designated space for all your teaching equipment, and this space should not interfere with any of the traffic patterns you have designed. Your main teaching space might be considered permanent for now (or at least semi-permanent), as it's not always practical to move your teaching easel or adjust and readjust a technology cart and screen every

◀ **Figure 1.26** First-grade classroom. Shayla used a swivel chair to easily move between a small-group teaching space and her teacher station. Notice how she also encouraged movement by adding kick bands to the bottoms of chairs so that more active students had the ability to move their feet while seated, which helped with concentration (Abdelbary 2017).

▶ **Figure 1.27** Fifth-grade classroom. Until her projector was mounted on the ceiling, Jamaica created her own flexible teaching space using a mobile whiteboard easel and a small technology station (she used strategic rug placement and JVCC Wire-Line Cable Cover Tape to keep students from tripping over cords). The layout for this whole-group meeting area matched the evolution in her teaching style, which became less about content delivery and more about student engagement.

time you teach a whole-group lesson. However, now there are portable whiteboards and easels that allow you to teach in different areas of the classroom. (See Figures 1.23–1.27.)

Willing to share your teacher work space during school hours? When you reimagine your room design, consider how much real estate your personal work space or desk takes up in the floor plan. Are you ready to ditch your large teacher desk? By sacrificing your desk, you can create another potential small-group work space for students. For teaching materials or supplies, designate a shelf or section of your storage closet that is easy to view and access.

If you would prefer to keep your desk, consider allowing students to use it as another option for individual or small-group work space. Or consider downsizing. Request a smaller desk and/or move it to a less central location, perhaps closer to a wall, doorway, or faraway corner.

Furniture Considerations: Incorporating Tech into Your Teacher Work Space

For some of us, technology now plays a big role in our teaching (e.g., document camera, PowerPoint presentations, videos, speakers, anything that might require a screen and space). Where will your tech tools be—on a mobile cart, desk, or shelf? Factor in proximity to outlets and students' ability to view the screen or board. No matter what you use, make sure your tools (pens, sticky notes, chart paper, notebooks) are stored nearby and are easily accessible.

Surrounding Spaces

WALLS

We often resign ourselves when it comes to the wall space. We get what we get. We inherit corkboards and whiteboards that are fastened to walls in classrooms that, over the years, may have been home to different grades. One year it was a fifth-grade classroom, the next it becomes an overflow kindergarten and first-second grade combination classroom. Learners today expect walls to be more interactive. They want to fully participate in their learning experiences. Using classroom walls as tools for collaboration—whiteboarding (idea generating), documenting growth (process board), as well as for displaying (products)—is key. Being creative and strategic with wall space improves student focus, engagement, and memorization. No more cookie-cutter displays. Use walls to push, grow, and stimulate thinking. (See Figures 1.28–1.30.)

Some rules of thumb to consider:

- Document and celebrate student learning. Share student work throughout different stages of the process. Encourage student input on what is and what is not displayed.

- Keep some of your wall space clear, perhaps as much as 20 percent to 50 percent, to decrease visual clutter and distraction.

- Connecting purpose to your wall space will help guide choices for color scheme and how student work and visual artifacts are displayed.

- Use neutral background colors like pastels, beige, or off-white hues to keep the focus on the work that is being displayed.

- Balance your wall spaces with student work and learning charts that support student independence and self-reliance (e.g., partnership resources, weekly book shopping schedule).

Figure 1.28 Kindergarten classroom. Rosanne dedicated one corner area of the classroom library to displaying the published works of her young writers. Readers could interact with the wall by removing the booklets that were suspended on clips and reading and leaving comments for classmates. She also attached a small, freestanding shelf to the wall to spotlight books connected to the current unit of study.

Figure 1.29 First-grade classroom. Rather than overload display boards and walls with the accumulation of student work across the year, Shayla sent projects and assignments home at regular intervals, keeping a variety of student art and documents that showcased each learner's process. She also made it a point to honor student work by keeping the areas around the walls clutter-free.

Figure 1.30 Second-grade classroom. A combination of neutral, blue, and gray hues were used on wall spaces to evoke feelings of calmness in this primary-grade classroom.

WINDOWS

If your classroom has windows, try to avoid covering them with charts, student work, or decorations. According to research, learners that work in classrooms where there is more natural light outperform students in math and literacy than those who are exposed to less natural light (Edwards and Torcelli 2002; Tanner 2008). If you do not have windows, be sure your room is well lit. When using technology, think about how you might alter your windows to control the flow of natural and/or artificial light through the use of shades, curtains, or a dimmer switch. (See Figures 1.31–1.32.)

Some rules of thumb to consider with windows and window coverings:

- Let in as much natural sunlight as you can, even if it's just part of the day.

- Be mindful of visual comfort; take measures to prevent uncomfortable sun glare.

- Do your best to block outside distractions without blocking the natural light. Use curtains, blinds, or creative window treatments.

- Be aware of the effects of natural sunlight on the temperature in the room and make adjustments, as needed.

Figures 1.31a and 1.31b Kindergarten classrooms. Rosanne and her next-door teaching partner Christine took full advantage of the natural light streaming in through the small windows of their inner-city classrooms. Small, inexpensive, potted indoor plants were placed around the room during the week and then perched near the window over the weekend.

Figure 1.32 Second-grade classroom. Although large windows overlooked a small garden and busy playground, the benefits of natural light outweighed any potential distractions.

STORAGE

Closets haunt many educators at home and at work. What to donate, what to toss, and what to keep? To save you from the hassle, why not include students in on the organizational tasks and upkeep? You may even consider removing the doors for easier visibility and accessibility of materials (Figures 1.33–1.35). I'd recommend you spend some time clearing everything out at the end of each year. I know you are exhausted in June, but you will thank yourself for doing it when you come back to school in August and are staring at clutter-free storage cabinets.

Some rules of thumb to consider with storage:

- If you did not use it in the past six months, donate it or toss it.
- Organize items that are alike or similar.
- Use transparent storage containers.
- Clearly label storage containers.
- Sort shelves by content, theme, season, and/or frequency of use.
- Position items you need for the day, week, and/or month in strategic ways (toward the front, side, etc.).

▶ **Figure 1.34** Third-grade classroom. Notice the proximity of math materials, counting collections, tools, and anchor charts in Jamaica's classroom that offered students opportunities to work independently and with plenty of resources to help themselves get unstuck when they encountered challenges.

▼ **Figure 1.33** Kindergarten classroom. The central station supply area that Rosanne created held tools for a writing workshop on the top level and a mix of art materials sorted into baskets in the compartment's bottom level. Even with all of the options to choose from, notice how the color and natural fibers of her storage containers contribute to a sense of organization and harmony.

▲ **Figure 1.35** Middle school classroom. Storage can be both functional and stylish. Aimee added to the aesthetic of the classroom by using a white wooden cabinet from home to store tech and supplies.

CORNERS

Corner classroom nooks are ideal spaces that support collaboration and differentiation (Figure 1.37). Corners can also be an oasis for students working alone (as seen in Figures 1.36a and 1.36b), in small groups, in peer partnerships, or for teacher-led small-group instruction.

Some rules of thumb to consider about corners:

- Design a large gathering space at the center of the classroom that allows you to keep corners free.

- Equip corners with their own storage units so students can retrieve and access materials.

- Corners have the potential to be contemplation and cool-down zones. Many learners find that they need a few minutes to think, breathe, troubleshoot, and self-regulate before continuing with learning.

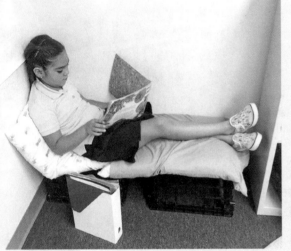

▲ **Figures 1.36a and 1.36b** Third-grade classroom. Evelyn and Albert made themselves at home while working in a quiet corner space. Corners are popular solo spots during independent work time.

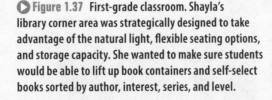

▶ **Figure 1.37** First-grade classroom. Shayla's library corner area was strategically designed to take advantage of the natural light, flexible seating options, and storage capacity. She wanted to make sure students would be able to lift up book containers and self-select books sorted by author, interest, series, and level.

Teaching into the Physical Environment

Imagine teaching at a new school but no one bothered to show you around the building or explained how things worked—where you should park, teacher supply room location, school lunchroom rituals? You'd feel pretty lost at first and it might take you longer than you'd like to feel comfortable. Well, even though many of our students have been in the school before, when they start a new school year, they're in a new environment. Usually they walk into a new classroom and don't know where things are or how things work. We don't often think about taking the time to teach students about the physical environment. When we plan the start of a new school year, we think about what we might read aloud, what community-building activity makes the most sense, and how we might launch reading, writing, math, science, or social studies. For everything to run as smoothly as possible and for students to maximize their learning, we'll also need to plan for and invest time in teaching about the physical environment—what's there, why it's there, and how it works.

What's there? Take your students on a brief tour of each of the classroom areas and allow them time to explore, rehearse, and become familiar with what each space has to offer. You'll especially want students to learn about the resources and supplies that are stored in each area.

Why is it there? When we talk with students about why a space, learning resource, or seating option is in the classroom, it allows learners to feel ownership and take responsibility over their own learning. When they know what is happening and the purpose for it, they can make better, informed decisions about where to sit, whom to sit next to, and what tools to use. Having this information also helps learners better understand the consequences of making decisions that lead to distractions, challenges with participation, or unproductivity.

How does it work? Teaching about how different spaces in the classroom work and how to effectively participate in each gives learners some guidelines or parameters about how to make the most of a given space. During community discussions, encourage students to voice any anxieties about where to sit or about the space itself. Invite learners to give regular and frequent feedback and to share any questions they have about the space. You'll need their help in the care and upkeep of each classroom area.

Here's an example of a lesson I might teach about the small-group spaces in our classroom, using the architecture of minilessons as defined by the Teachers College Reading and Writing Project (Calkins 2003).

A SAMPLE LESSON: GETTING TO KNOW OUR CLASSROOM LAYOUT (THIRD GRADE)
Connection (3–4 minutes)

If you have ever been to a fair or amusement park, site operators often provide a guide or map to show folks where important places on the grounds are located and what you will find in the space when you get there. This guide is sometimes designed by using a bird's-eye view perspective, from overhead, so that you can see everything easily and in relation to other areas. Here is an example of an amusement park map. (Place the map brochure on the document camera.) I took some aerial photos of our classroom to try and provide some of the same information about our classroom layout as fair operators would give to their patrons. One goal

Figures 1.38a and 1.38b As part of the minilesson, Jamica's students worked with a partner or trio to explore classroom spaces. They used this photo guide sheet and checklist as they toured each space. They also took notes and jotted questions about each of the areas before returning to the lesson for a whole-class discussion.

for our lesson today is to become familiar with the classroom layout so that you are able to have a picture in mind of where you think you might be able to do your best work. I'd like to introduce you to some of the learning spaces created especially for you. First, we'll study the space in a two-dimensional form using a photo so that we can practice together how to notice and think about each space and what it has to offer. Then you'll have a chance after the lesson to step into and explore each space so that you can feel its size, touch the items you are curious about, and learn how its design and organization will support peer collaboration.

Teach (3–5 minutes)

Here is a photo guide of all of our classroom spaces. (I place the photo in Figure 1.38a on the document camera next to the Classroom Layout Checklist in Figure 1.38b.) *Watch me closely as I study the photo of the classroom library space by moving my finger across the image, scanning it from left to right. Listen as I notice, name, and check off what I observe in the space. I'll also imagine myself using the space and thinking about questions I want to ask. Lastly, I'll use this checklist to check off items and jot down any questions I have.*

(I begin my demonstration by looking at the image of the classroom library that is displayed on the document camera.) *OK, so I notice a few things right away. I see that it has a large rug, lots of books, a huge window, bookshelves, a floor lamp, small table, and different kinds of seating. I can totally see myself choosing a book and sitting in this camp chair next to the window. One thing I am wondering about this space is if it would be OK to sit under the table and read.* (I model stopping and jotting the question on my checklist. Then I check off other items I see in the space.)

(If you think students need to see you demonstrate with another classroom space, go ahead. If you think heading over to the actual space in the classroom and demonstrating your thinking and how to use the checklist inside of the space itself would be more effective, go for it. I decided to use an image with this grade level so that everyone would be focused on the process of studying a space and jotting down ideas rather than be distracted by the space itself and everyone trying to fit in it. For older students, I would likely demonstrate this lesson in the actual space by gathering students there and leading a quick chat before inviting them to explore the space in teams or pods.)

Active Engagement (2–4 minutes)

Now you and your partner will work together to study another image of our classroom. Visualize yourself in the space and notice and name out what you see. Share any questions that you have. Go ahead and try it. (Give partners a few minutes to name out what they see and to list any questions they may have about the space. While partners are chatting, rotate around the meeting area to support student conversations as needed.)

Closing (1–2 minutes)

(Bring everyone back together). *We've now had an opportunity to take a brief two-dimensional tour of some of our classroom spaces and notice and wonder about some of the items and resources featured in each part of the classroom. One goal of this lesson is to start to become familiar with the classroom layout so that you are able to have a picture in mind of where you think you might be able to do your best thinking and problem solving. It will take some time to rotate through each of the classroom spaces today and see what they have to offer. Be sure and "try on" each space to see which ones connect with you and allow you to work in ways that feel the most productive to your learning style.*

Now, you'll divide into teams to explore each section of the classroom space for approximately three to five minutes. Use this checklist to guide your observations. Then you and your team will rotate clockwise to the next section when you hear the signal. As you spend time in each space, be sure to make yourself comfortable, look around, sit down, notice amenities, and discuss with a partner any questions that come to mind. If you have any wonderings or questions for me or suggestions on how to improve the space, jot those down too. OK, let's begin. I look forward to hearing your thoughts.

(Once teams are established, pass out a checklist and then set a timer for each rotation. Meet back together in the whole-group meeting area after students have had the chance to rotate through each classroom area you'd like to spotlight. Briefly close the lesson by sharing comments, questions, and suggestions about each of the spaces. Document the process so that you can revisit it again in the near future and chart improvements or challenges.)

A QUICK GUIDE TO LAYOUT

Learning Space

WHOLE-GROUP MEETING SPACE

Some Possible Visual Resources

Elements

Large open area

Flexible seating options

Teaching tools:

- whiteboard

- tech cart

- computer

- document camera

- Smart Board

- audio system

Purpose

To create a centralized teaching and learning space that also nurtures interpersonal relationships

Participation Opportunities

Taking turns

Exchanging ideas

Taking risks

Asking questions

Reflecting as a whole group

Self-evaluating

Applying new learning

Some Possible Teaching Ideas

Designing arrival and departure guidelines

Finding space/choosing a seat

Sharing ideas with the whole group

Sharing ideas with a partner

Using thinking tools

flexible seating choices

stool

crate

balance ball

chair

Learning Space
SMALL-GROUP WORK SPACE

Some Possible Visual Resources

Elements

Accommodates 4–5 students at a time

Flexible seating options

Variety of writing surfaces

Purpose

To create a relatively small space away from the larger meeting area

To provide opportunities to collaborate with teacher or peers on assignments, typically with differentiated support

Participation Opportunities

Work collaboratively

Think aloud

Set group and personal goals

Exchange ideas

Collectively complete tasks

Self-evaluate

Receive feedback

Give feedback

Take more risks

Ask more questions

Apply new learning

Some Possible Teaching Ideas

Designing arrival and departure guidelines

Finding space for yourself

Choosing a seating option

Sharing ideas with a partner

Using thinking tools

Troubleshooting challenges

Generating lots of possible solutions

Learning how to be a flexible partner

Learning how to be a compassionate partner

Our Classroom Spaces

Classroom Library | Math Corner and Supply Area

Whole Group Meeting Area | Small Group Area and Writing Supply Station

Coffee Table and Exploration Table | Central Supply Stations

Classroom Layout Checklist and Observations

Name | Date

Name of Work Area:

What I notice about... | What it makes me think or questions I have:

Seating | Seating
☐ School chairs
☐ Arm chairs
☐ Stools
☐ Swivel Chairs
☐ Crates
☐ Benches
☐ Balance balls
☐ Other

Surfaces | Surfaces
☐ Individual desks
☐ Tables
☐ Coffee table
☐ Whiteboard table
☐ Standing desk
☐ Tray table
☐ Other

Supplies | Supplies
☐ Pencils/Pens
☐ Colored Pencils
☐ Markers
☐ Paper
☐ Post-its
☐ Clips
☐ Other

Other | Other

Learning Space

INDIVIDUAL WORK SPACES

Elements

Accommodates one learner at time

Situated away from frequent interruptions, distractions, or loud talking

Flexible seating options

Variety of writing surfaces

Purpose

To create a space for independent project work away from large- or small-group meeting areas

Participation Opportunities

Practice independently

Set personal goals

Complete tasks

Self-evaluate

Take risks

Receive feedback

Apply new learning

Some Possible Teaching Ideas

Designing arrival and departure guidelines

Finding space and seating options

Determining what to do when the space I want to work in is unavailable

Learning how to
  - set goals
  - self-manage
  - self-regulate

CARE AND MAINTENANCE

Classroom upkeep is much too big a responsibility for a few monitors and table captains or for the teacher alone. If the classroom learning goals are centered around instruction, everyone needs to pitch in. According to Stronge, Tucker, and Hindman (2004, 64), "Effective teachers expertly manage and organize the classroom and expect their students to contribute in a positive and productive manner. It seems prudent to pay careful attention to classroom climate, given that it can have as much impact on student learning as student aptitude (Wang, Haertel, and Walberg, 1993[/1994])." Most often, the custodial staff does an incredible job getting classrooms to look their best before the school year begins. When school is in session, however, most of the day-to-day maintenance belongs to the teacher. Ways to build agreements around classroom upkeep is to have a whole-group discussion about health (including the brain) and hygiene.

1.) Rinse your hands

2.) Put on soap

3.) Wash all the soap off

4.) Dry your hands really well both sides front & back

Take time to brainstorm expectations together, make a plan with shared goals, divide up the cleaning and organizing tasks in equitable ways, and be sure to allow students plenty of opportunities to practice, practice, practice. Create checklists as well as daily, weekly, and monthly schedules to measure effectiveness and ensure accountability.

Classroom Maintenance Checklist

Week of _____

	Completed by:				
	M	T	W	Th	F
Pick up trash					
Sweep floor					
Wipe off tables					
Return materials to location					

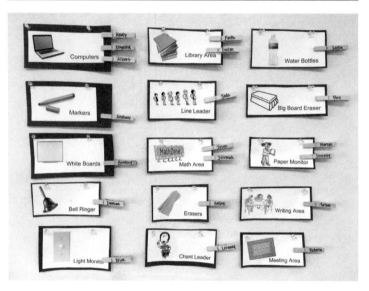

No matter what grade you teach, it's important for learners to establish and practice good hygiene habits and to also apply those habits when they are in the classroom. Something as simple as regular and proper handwashing is a really big deal and affects the health of an entire community. As a constant reminder, consider posting a simple handwashing routine by the sink area.

IF–THEN SCENARIOS

I like all of these ideas, but I am physically unable to move my furniture around or my administration will not let me change out furniture. What can I do to reimagine the layout of my classroom to support more positive learning behaviors?

There are other things you might consider besides changing out the furniture in your classroom. Creating a variety of learning areas that allow students to make choices about where they can think and learn best can be a great place to start with the furniture you already have. Start small; designate one or two individual spaces around your room for those who need a quieter place to work. In Chapter 4, you'll learn more about some other design elements that are influential in supporting classroom behaviors, student motivation, and learning. For example, the use of natural light and reducing outside sound (noise) seem to have a larger impact on student learning than once thought. Also, the latest thinking about limiting the use of color could also be a place to start with your redesign efforts. "It appears easier to over-stimulate students with vibrant colors and busy displays, than to create calm but interesting environments suitable for learning" (Barrett et al. 2013).

If I give my students more choice about where they work, then how will I be able to control their productivity and behavior?

Learning that incorporates student choice is a very powerful pathway to ensuring more productivity and engagement. Increasing opportunities that allow students to make choice decreases off-task behaviors. When students take part in the decision-making process (for example, where they work, what they work on, and how they accomplish the task), they are more invested in the outcome, which generally leads to higher-quality and

math supplies

math supplies

pattern blocks

base ten blocks

collections

base ten blocks

collections

unfix cubes

collections

more meaningful work. Participating in their own learning design also gives students an opportunity to be more accountable for their learning, which allows you to feel less stress about being in control. From the start, students will be learning how to set goals, develop timelines, make plans, and self-evaluate—all with your continuous strategic feedback.

If I have accumulated lots of resources over the years, how do I hold on to all of the things I like to use with the kids and also have clutter-free spaces?

If you haven't used materials or resources that are taking up valuable real estate in the classroom (including closet space) in meaningful ways in the last six months, then it is considered clutter. For classrooms to be optimal places of learning for students, you will have to make decisions about the resources you have acquired over the years. Donate, toss out, or store items elsewhere that do not directly impact student opportunities for learning. Take small steps by working on one shelf or drawer at a time. It will feel so good.

If I want to give my students makerspace opportunities, where does that fit in my layout?

Students now see themselves as creators and designers. Maybe your school has an innovation lab or a learning studio. Even if it doesn't, you might want to carve out a simple makerspace in your classroom so that you can promote and encourage design thinking. You'll only need a work surface (use existing tables, whole-group area, or counter space) and a storage container to hold materials for use with small projects.

2

Making Sure Every Classroom Space Enhances Teaching and Learning

Jade, a former third-grade student, often preferred to sit and work away from classmates during independent work time. She complained about the ambient noise from her peers and desperately wanted to create a space for herself near the front of the classroom where it seemed quieter. I gave her the OK, and she spread out her supplies and worked on the floor just under the whiteboard. Later in the year, Jade asked for a desk in that exact spot. Soon it became like a personal office space. I noticed that Jade chose to work in this personal office space when she really wanted to practice, try something new, or complete a project on her own. She was connected to herself as a learner and knew what kind of space she needed. It was Jade who inspired me most to think about how important individual spaces in the classroom can be for learners.

Every person needs a place that is furnished with hope.

—MAYA ANGELOU,
*THE OXFORD BOOK
OF AMERICAN
LIGHT VERSE*

When students have opportunities to revisit, make connections to, and manipulate new learning, rather than just be drilled and tested on it, they have a better chance to retain information. "Active students have the opportunity to shape the learning experience to their specific needs . . . Relative to passive observation, our review suggests that active control has positive effects on memory across a wide range of activities and student populations" (Markant et al., 146–9). "Mentally manipulating new and already known information increases memory and understanding, so providing learners multiple ways to apply their learning in new applications or situations helps their brains build increasing awareness of the concepts behind that new information. These mental

manipulations guide students to progress from an initial concrete fact to more abstract conceptual knowledge" (Willis 2018). Creating spaces for learners in the classroom with the purpose of revisiting new learning in multiple ways actually develops mental pathways to long-term memory storage in the hippocampus. Research shows that students perform more efficiently and better academically when they have repeated opportunities to review learned material (Kang 2016).

Learners like Jade need time and space to revisit content and to practice skills and strategies that are targeted toward their development. Ideally, learners are in on the process and can help make some of the decisions about what works best for them in the space.

Making Every Classroom Space Work for Students

When and where do your students have repeated opportunities to review learned material? In addition to your whole-group, small-group, and individual work areas, your classroom has other spaces you'll need to consider and plan for. Although each classroom has a unique design, many teachers maximize learning by taking advantage of walls, perimeters, and corner spaces. These spaces can serve as an oasis to flex thinking and talking muscles, or as quieter zones for learners to tune out distractions. Some of the more popular "other" classroom spaces are often dual or multipurpose areas and feature a classroom library, a multimedia learning space, makerspace, and an art atelier. No matter what additional areas you decide to include in the layout of your classroom, it's important to create opportunities for learners to interact with the space. In other words, how are we designing each space to foster collaboration and maximize student learning potential? And which spaces might motivate students to engage with learning in ways that help them accomplish their content, language, and behavior goals?

If your class has a flair for the dramatic arts, then why not find ways to incorporate playwriting and improvisational work into your curriculum? Imagine moving a few desks out of the way, hanging a curtain, and carving out a theatre-like space for performances and presentations in one corner of your classroom.

If your students like to tinker, then be sure to incorporate opportunities and space to dismantle or reverse engineer appliances. Tinkering can develop fine motor skills and problem-solving abilities and promote language and positive peer relationships. To get started, all you need is a work surface, a few storage containers, a shelf space, and a wall space to display plans, prototype drawings, and resources. "The long-term benefits of tinkering time are remarkable," says Katy Scott, Education Technology Specialist. "In many ways, tinkering resembles inquiry-based learning, cooperative learning, and project-based learning, all of which have been proven to have long-term positive effects on student achievement and success" (Scott 2010).

When you think about creating a classroom environment for all students, be sure that supplies, resources, and technology are available and adaptable to the learning needs of your diverse learning community. Most classrooms have students with a unique range of academic, social, and emotional learning needs, so it will be important to teach students how to independently access resources they may want to use to support their learning goals.

Classroom Libraries

Strategically organized classroom libraries are now commonplace in many K–8 classrooms. Educators and parent teams have spent countless hours sorting texts by topic, interest, author, genre, and reading level as needed so that students can more easily find books that connect with their passion and interests. Classroom library spaces can serve multiple purposes—they can be a resource for information, a small-group work space, and a refuge to those students

▼ **Figures 2.1a and 2.1b** First-grade classroom library. Shayla kept visibility and accessibility in mind. Notice how books were sorted, labeled, and displayed using lightweight, transparent bins. Alfonso could easily go to the section he was interested in, sort through the options, and choose exactly what he wanted to read by interest and/or level. By arranging the library along the perimeter of the classroom, students could sit inside of the space and enjoy books using a variety of soft seating options, including beanbag chairs.

◀ **Figure 2.2** Fifth-grade classroom library. Although the view from the window was of a busy playground, Jamica wanted her library space in a corner and was determined to keep the blinds open to bring in natural light. Gradually, as students got used to the view, it became a nonissue. The library corner quickly became a favorite space to quietly finish up assignments.

◀ **Figure 2.3** Middle school classroom library. Aimee's library lined the perimeter of one wall. She designed her own checkout system using a book-leveling app. Her students could borrow books from the class library by scanning their ID card and the book's barcode.

Figure 2.4 Kindergarten library. Rosanne carefully organized and curated this corner area to invite readers into the comfy library space and to display and interact with texts written by classmates. Notice the student-written booklets clipped to the wall. Her library also doubled as a small-group teaching space.

who enjoy getting lost in books and making choices about what they read. When you imagine a practical and engaging classroom library, think about how much space you need. Consider the age and size of your readers and the number of books you have. The space you designate should be big enough for students to easily access a variety of books and spacious enough to include a small group of readers who choose to remain in the library area to read or work. (See Figures 2.1–2.4.)

Furniture Considerations: Library

When furnishing your library, start with a few shelves or cabinets and then add more cabinets as your library grows and changes with your readers. Consider the type of shelving options you have and the size of storage bins. You don't want them to become too heavy or hard to lift. Often teachers will frame the library space with the bookshelves, so students can sit in the middle to select books and read. As always, it's not necessary to have a rug in your library space. Think about what purpose a rug would serve and whether you can keep it clean.

Always consider the height of your students when designing your classroom library. Make sure each student can reach all the books. If you have book bins, make sure the weight is manageable. Students should be able to remove them to make book selections and then replace them back to their spot on the shelf. Some educators spend time making sure their libraries are organized and inviting. You might include different kinds of lighting, rugs, pillows, and tables to create a warm and welcoming space for learners.

Multimedia Learning Spaces

Today's learning spaces can go way beyond the four walls of the classroom. More schools are utilizing federal funding sources like Title I, grants, and donations to equip classrooms with technology (often arriving in charging carts). Many schools have moved away from computer labs and are asking students to bring in their own devices. When you think about integrating educational technology into your classroom environment, there are the practical concerns like adding

◀ ▲ **Figures 2.5a, 2.5b, 2.5c** Fourth-grade multimedia learning spaces. Lori's student tech team organized and managed the classroom digital device checkout system. The rotating tech team helped classmates check out devices, troubleshooted technology glitches, and connected devices to the charging cart at the close of the day. All learners had opportunities to integrate technology across the day, whether it was at their desks or in smaller collaborative configurations. Students used Google Classroom and other educational apps to research information, design projects, practice skills, and take assessments.

▲ **Figure 2.6** Fifth-grade multimedia learning space. Fifth graders congregated around a whiteboard laminate surface table with write-on/wipe-off functionality. They enjoyed the opportunity to use both physical pens and digital devices as they learned how to design and create games during a small-group coding session.

▶ **Figure 2.7** Middle school teacher multimedia learning space and charging cart. Aimee set up the classroom digital tools and teaching space on carts in the front of the room. She even created a small wall nook to hang and preserve headsets. She also put in a work order to mount her projector on the ceiling to save space. Since she incorporated flexible seating choices, she found herself teaching less from the front of the room. With the help of technology, it felt more natural to circulate around the room and teach from different areas when she needed to deliver information or share a strategy with students.

outlets or power strips to power more devices (outlets in classrooms are elusive and having a few more would be awesome!). More importantly, you'll want to think about whether the classroom environment is conducive to meaningful collaborative and interactive experiences. Some educators experiment by moving desks out of rows, so students can work in pods that mirror the small-group collaborative structures in today's workforce. (See Figures 2.5–2.7.)

Here are some initial rules of thumb to consider when you strategically design spaces that support multimedia learning and connectivity in the physical classroom:

- Location of electrical outlets—identify where devices can be stored and charged.

- Location of internet access— be aware of spots in your building or classroom with poor internet access.

- Maintenance and location—position devices away from chalk dust, water, and magnets.

- Number of devices—consider how many students can be in the multimedia learning space at one time.

- Time limits—make sure every student has the same minimum amount of time with devices.

Refer to Figures 2.8 and 2.9 for additional information on tech tools and software or apps.

Figure 2.8 Tech Tools to Consider

Basic Tech Tools to Consider	Suggestions
Electronic Devices Laptop, tablet, smartphone, watch	Portable devices like laptops and tablets can be used anywhere but are best used on a flat surface like a desk or table. Make sure to clear an area next to electronic devices so there is room for a notebook or note-taking.
Printer An electronic device that processes stored data from a computer or other external device and generates a replica on physical media	Consider a tech cart dedicated to your printer that has mobile capabilities and would allow you to stack your print technology for more space and greater flexibility.
Projector A classroom staple that displays a mirrored video output from an external device on any flat surface and can be used with lots of different devices by both teachers and students	Mount your projector to save valuable floor space. (Put in a service request order ASAP!) Consider your lighting zones. You'll want areas near the projector to be darker and areas near learners to be brighter, so they can more easily transition from the screen to their work.

Basic Tech Tools to Consider	Suggestions
Projection Screen/Flat Screen Monitor Screens that enable all students to see digital information on a flat surface	Adjust screens so that the bottom is approximately five feet from the ground. Ensure it is visible to everyone. Every learner should be able to see the screen no matter where they are in the classroom.
SMART Boards Touch-sensitive whiteboards that allow learners to interact with digital content, use digital markers, keep a record of what is written, and mirror your computer screen	Clear a path for a walk-up space near the SMART Board. Learners need to be able to interact with the SMART Board at the ground level, so they can manipulate images during a discussion, or guide an online inquiry.
Document Camera A digital machine that projects images and artifacts by capturing them with its camera; a practical device for presenting on-the-go information to a large group	Position a document camera in a place where students have easy access. You will want to be sure that students learn how to effectively use the document camera for presentations and to support thinking.
Physical Storage Shelving, cabinets, containers, electronic charging station (ECS)	Set up and store devices so they are located in one place for both practicality and security purposes. Using a mobile cart tech system allows for easy retrieval and helps maximize space. Consider an ECS system that stores and charges batteries in the devices simultaneously. They come in different shapes and sizes and help eliminate cord and cable clutter.
Cloud Storage Internet storage that can store classroom documents and assignments, allow teachers to put information online for their learners, as well as let teachers collect and grade student work online	There are tools educators commonly use to organize documents and files in the cloud. Onebox, Dropbox, and Google Drive are the most common boxes. Google Drive is the most popular since it's free, has ample online storage, and allows you to share files with students so they can access and work on projects and documents during school hours and outside of the classroom.
Embedded Cameras Most come readily installed in laptops, desktops, and tablets; offer a variety of learning opportunities using Microsoft's Skype in the Classroom	Review digital citizenship guidelines with students prior to using cameras as there are privacy rules to agree upon and abide by. Cameras should only be used to record themselves or others as part of their learning task or project. After filming, students will often need a digital space and software to view their work, collaborate with peers to identify areas for improvement, and edit their projects.

Figure 2.9 Software and Apps

Software or App	How They Support Learning and Collaboration
Google Classroom **Google Apps for Education** • Google Drive • Google Docs • Google Spreadsheet • Google Calendars • Google Forms • Google Expeditions An online website platform that helps manage and streamline communication, productivity, and idea and resource sharing between teachers and students	Google Classroom is an application that allows teachers to easily manage their workload inside and outside of the classroom. It can serve as a central hub of communication for teachers, students, and parents. It fully integrates with all Google Apps for Education to help students and teachers share information, stay organized, and participate in online discussions together. Students can create their own Google Drive folder to upload their work, then share and receive comments and feedback from peers and teachers during different stages of the project or task.
Book Creator An app that allows you and your students to create and publish your own digital texts	Learners can author or co-author their own how-to books and manuals, comic strips, poetry anthologies, graphic novels, science, and history chapter books. They can also assemble digital portfolios that highlight examples of student or group work from across the school year. This app also provides opportunities for emergent bilingual students to build language skills through digital storytelling.
EDpuzzle An annotation tool that allows you to personalize and differentiate video content (Khan Academy, TED, NPR, Nat Geo, etc.) for each of your learners in strategic ways	Learners can go at their own pace as they use this app to view new or review learned material by themselves or with peers. You can insert you own audio notes, links, images, and questions that prompt learners to stop, think, jot, and process information alone, with partners, or in small groups at various intervals.
Flipgrid An app that allows you and your students to pose a question or prompt to an audience and then share the results or information collected	Learners can respond to questions or ideas with short video recordings of themselves. They can also respond to each other's videos. Some possible ideas for student assignments might include generate book reviews, questions about a content-area topic of study, explain and justify math strategies, share prototype ideas for projects.
NewseumED An online platform for media literacy education that includes tools for evaluating primary and secondary resources, digital artifacts, collections, films, and exhibits; also includes lesson plan tools and ideas organized by topic and time period	Learners, especially English language arts and history students, can develop critical thinking skills through the reading, analysis, and discussion of informational text from multiple print and digital sources. The virtual format sparks discussion and collaboration in deep and meaningful ways. It also offers tools to help students learn how to differentiate news from noise.

Furniture Considerations: Multimedia Learning Spaces

Figures 2.10a, 2.10b, 2.10c, 2.10d, 2.10e Classrooms from grades 1 to 8. When it comes to multimedia learning spaces, consider acquiring portable lap desks to use as surfaces, since most students prefer to read sitting in something other than straight-backed chairs. Portable lap desks can be used while on the floor, couch, crate—almost any seating option. Finally, keep things organized and clutter-free by including an area for lap desk storage so students can easily retrieve items they need and then return them when they're finished. It's helpful that there are lots of storage systems for every purpose and budget.

Makerspaces

Makerspaces are collaborative areas where students are encouraged to be curious, creative, and innovative. A makerspace typically has an assortment of materials and tools to help learners accomplish their DIY design goals. Older students like to be involved with the actual design of the space as well as make suggestions and help collect materials that will be included. Since learners are embracing their newfound identities as creators and designers, you'll no doubt want a space to help them imagine the unimaginable, tinker, create, design, and build prototypes. The small makerspace can be used for DIY projects of choice or to support a content-area learning goal. "For older students, making combines disciplines in ways that enhance the learning process for diverse student populations and opens doors to unforeseen career paths" (Martinez and Stager 2013, 3). Makerspaces provide opportunities for students to pursue passion projects that deepen their understanding of their community and the world, develop empathy for others, and promote activism. "When we allow children to experiment, take risks, and play with their own ideas, we give them permission to trust themselves. They begin to see themselves as learners who have good ideas and can transform their own ideas into reality" (Martinez and Stager 2013, 36). (See Figures 2.11–2.13.)

Maybe your school already has an innovation lab or learning studio. Even if it does, you can still carve out a small makerspace area in your classroom to promote and encourage design thinking. It's easy to get started! You'll need a place to store all your materials and tools and a space for your students to create. It will be easier than you think to gather materials. Traditional spaces have crafting and art supplies; recyclable and repurposed materials; building materials; traditional tools like scissors, rulers, and tape measures; and, if possible, industrial tools like rechargeable electric drills and screwdrivers.

Next think about how and when students will access this area. Most teachers like to have their classroom makerspace available during content-area science and social studies time or at the end of the day, but don't limit yourself or your kids. Empower learners to take ownership of their learning by requesting and scheduling time to work in this space; perhaps they might even create a print or online sign-up sheet. There's also a good chance your learners will come up with an idea for how and when to use the makerspace you didn't anticipate!

◀ **Figure 2.12**
Third-grade classroom. Clearing off tabletop space easily turns a classroom into a makerspace gallery during an open house or for a back-to-school night showcase. Invite parents and visitors from other classrooms and have students present their ideas, process, and projects to admiring and inquisitive audiences.

▲ ▶ **Figures 2.11a, 2.11b, 2.11c, 2.11d**
Classrooms from grades 1 to 8. There is no right way to set up a makerspace; teachers use tables, cabinets, shelves, carts, different-sized storage containers, and cubbies to organize and manage resources as well as to keep the classroom space tidy.

▲ **Figure 2.13** Third-grade classroom. Once you have collected an assortment of tools and repurposed materials, the fun and hands-on learning can begin with maker-inspired STEAM (science, technology, engineering, art, and mathematics) activities and projects. Jamaica's third graders worked in teams one afternoon to explore Newton's second law of motion. They constructed inclined planes and used balls and cars to learn about the concepts of force, mass, and acceleration.

Content-Area Spaces

Potentially any area around the classroom can serve as a home base for storing and displaying content-related inquiry studies. In this space, students have increased opportunities to make sense of new learning and to interact with a variety of realia, helping them develop a deeper understanding of a theme or topic. It will be important for learners to have tools to keep track of

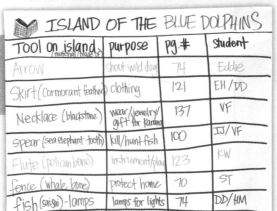

Figures 2.14a, 2.14b, 2.14c, 2.14d Classrooms from grades 3 to 4. Designated exploration and inquiry tables, like the one in Angela's class, are perfect places to gather provisions like text sets, maps, costumes, photographs, artifacts, and primary resources that will support your science and social studies provocations, investigations, and curricular goals. Students can research and sketch out ideas, then create and display projects they designed to showcase their learning. Students can even bring over their digital devices to sit and conduct research.

ISLAND OF THE BLUE DOLPHINS

Tool on island (material/made of)	purpose	pg.#	Student
Arrow	shoot wild dog	74	Eddie
Skirt (cormorant feather)	clothing	121	EH/DD
Necklace (blackstone)	wear/jewelry/gift for Karana	137	VF
Spear (sea elephant tooth)	kill/hunt fish	100	IJ/VF
Flute (pelican bone)	Instrument/play	123	KW
fence (whale bone)	protect home	70	ST
fish (saisai)-lamps	lamps for lights	74	DD/HM
Knife (stone)	scraping hide	34	DD/MH

their wonderings and questions about a topic, identify problems and design solutions, document and display new learning. Some resources you might consider adding to a content-area space include topic-related texts, primary and secondary resources, 3D artifacts, magnifying glasses, digital devices, and note-taking materials. (See Figures 2.14–2.15.)

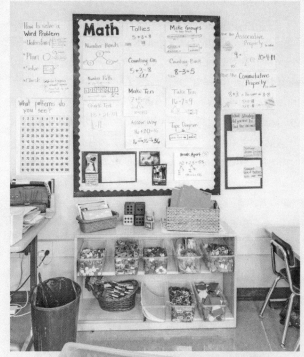

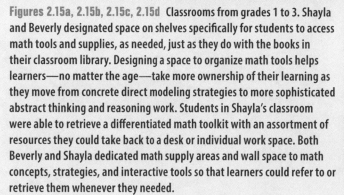

Figures 2.15a, 2.15b, 2.15c, 2.15d Classrooms from grades 1 to 3. Shayla and Beverly designated space on shelves specifically for students to access math tools and supplies, as needed, just as they do with the books in their classroom library. Designing a space to organize math tools helps learners—no matter the age—take more ownership of their learning as they move from concrete direct modeling strategies to more sophisticated abstract thinking and reasoning work. Students in Shayla's classroom were able to retrieve a differentiated math toolkit with an assortment of resources they could take back to a desk or individual work space. Both Beverly and Shayla dedicated math supply areas and wall space to math concepts, strategies, and interactive tools so that learners could refer to or retrieve them whenever they needed.

Art Atelier

Atelier is the French word for "studio" or "workshop" and was first incorporated by Italian educator Loris Malaguzzi into the Reggio Emilia model of early childhood development education in Italy, just after World War II. Traditionally the atelier plays a key role in each student's journey of knowledge and is designed and organized to foster imagination, creativity, and ownership of learning. In today's classrooms, art supplies and materials are generally relegated to the back of closets or under cobweb-filled classroom sinks. Consider designing your own art atelier. Openly storing and displaying art supplies in beautiful, thoughtful ways encourages both students and teachers to use them more often. It signifies the importance of art integration as a tool for expressing creativity and making meaning to gain deeper understandings of concepts. (See Figures 2.16a–d.)

Dedicating a space inside the classroom for art supplies and allowing students time and access to them may take some getting used to. The results may even encourage and inspire educators to incorporate more art into their daily routines. Wouldn't that be amazing! Start small. Begin by locating and updating art supplies, tossing out any old paints, dried-up markers, bits of crayon, or fraying paintbrushes. Sharpen your colored pencils and have students become familiar with the class art inventory by helping sort and organize your supplies, into bins, baskets, or jars. Put out some paper, and voilà, your art atelier is open. Teach into its use and upkeep by encouraging learners to visit the area often and adhering to the retrieval system that gives them ample chances to use the materials and practice putting them away.

Figures 2.16a, 2.16b, 2.16c, 2.16d Classrooms from grades 1 to 8. Short on space? Maximize it by creating art zones or an atelier where students can quickly retrieve materials from baskets, jars, and platters. Keep supplies visible to encourage learners to incorporate art into their projects and tasks, when applicable, to demonstrate deeper meaning and understanding.

55

Playful Spaces

Why not designate a space for play? Most experts agree that a key component to learning is play and that establishing a culture and space for play-based learning opportunities promotes whole-child development and positive social interactions between peers. It also provides learners with authentic ways to transfer their learning both alone and collaboratively. "Google gives employees space to be playful and play acts as a 'powerful motivator' for learning" (Heppell, Heppell, and Heppell 2015). Play in the classroom may look different in primary, intermediate, and middle school classrooms, but no matter the age, play also reduces stress, improves mood, and can encourage peer collaboration. Consider carving out a space for block building and dramatic play realia around a theme, like community or adaptations. In the intermediate and middle school grades, a table or rug space to meet up and play is still essential. Cards, board games, chess, jigsaw puzzles and Rubik's cubes can relieve tension, spark conversation and laughter, and provide endless opportunities to rehearse and practice conflict resolution and problem-solving skills (Figures 2.17a–d). "Play helps teams work together effectively and creates meaningful learning engagement" (Heppell, Heppell, and Heppell 2015).

Figures 2.17a, 2.17b, 2.17c, 2.17d Classrooms from grades 1 to 8. Spaces to think, problem-solve, and collaborate over puzzles and board games, blocks, and dramatic-play items are all part of a well-thought-out plan to relieve stress, spark creativity, and engage in creative play and social interaction.

Teaching into Every Classroom Space

You will want to properly introduce any space you and your students decide to design and create in a way that gives students a chance to grow familiar with it. During a class tour meeting, teach students about why the space was created, then brainstorm together about the roles and responsibilities in the space. This is also an opportunity for learners to seek out answers to their questions and make suggestions about how to improve upon the space. Once learners understand how to work and care for the space with independence, you will be able to focus more on how to use the space to provide differentiated and multisensory learning opportunities.

Here are examples of two lessons I might teach using the architecture of minilessons defined by the Teachers College Reading and Writing Project (Calkins 2003).

A SAMPLE LESSON: TEACHING INTO THE CLASSROOM LIBRARY

Connection (2–4 minutes)

Where is your favorite place to read anything you like outside of school? Go ahead close your eyes and take a minute to picture it in your mind. Maybe it's in your home, outside on a porch or patio, or perhaps it's in a car or bus on the way to school. Open your eyes. Now, it's my turn. I'm picturing my reading spot and thinking about why it's my favorite place to read. Well, it's in my home, in a comfy chair near a window. My fave place to read also has a small table nearby to hold my book and glass of water or coffee if I get thirsty. Quickly tell your partner about what you are picturing in your reading spot and why it is your favorite place to read. (Invite students to share their thoughts.)

Thanks for thinking and for sharing with your partner about what makes your reading spot so memorable. We are meeting around our classroom library space today because I'm hoping that this area might also become one of your favorite reading spots. I'd like to give you a little tour of the library so that you know what's in it, how it works, and your job or role as a reader while you are using the space on your "book shopping" day and during independent reading time. Then each of you will have a chance to explore the library on your own and share any thoughts, ideas, and questions you have about the area and, of course, suggestions on how to make the space even better.

Let's get started. Let's meet by the bookshelves in the library.

Teach (3–5 minutes)

First, I'd like to show you the different parts of the library. Currently in our library we have two mobile shelves, book bins, a rug area, a coffee table and lamp, a wall space, and a big picture window. (Highlight by standing near, pointing to, and/or picking up different parts of the library area, as needed.)

Now I'd like to talk a little about each of the parts, their purpose in the library space, and how to use them. We have two book cabinets that are on wheels. Each has three tiers of shelving. If you need to move the shelves around a bit to create a little more space in the corners, please go right ahead. Each mobile cabinet also holds book bins that are currently organized by topic, genre, or level to make books easier to find what you are looking for. Each book has a dot or label that lets you know which book bin it belongs to so that you know where (which bin) and how (front cover facing out) to return the book when you are finished reading it. There is a "book hospital" bin for any books that are damaged and need repair. Simply drop the book and any missing pages into this bin.

Next is the rug area, chairs, coffee table, and lamp. There are a few seating options and you are welcome to spread out on the rug and use chairs, crates, and any other seat while in the library. There is a small coffee table and lamp to use if you'd like. When you are finished using any of the seating options, simply return them to their space outside of the classroom library area.

Next, we have a wall space area that will be dedicated to charts and resources that you can use when you need a reminder about how to use the space or if you get stuck as a reader.

If you find a book and are not sure where it goes, use the dot or label on the outside cover to match the book to its bin. If there is no dot and it's a leveled book, you can also look inside of the back cover to find its guided reading book level and return it that way or put it in the book hospital so we can put a new dot label on it.

Voice level in the classroom and in the library is soft and low; whispering is encouraged so that we respect the work others are doing nearby to make meaning in their texts.

Moving slowly around the library is also recommended. Since it's not a very big space and folks are in different spots, be sure to pay attention to where you set up for reading so that you don't block access to any of the shelves or spread your books out all over the floor space, making it hard for others to move around.

Active Engagement: Guided Inquiry (2–4 minutes)

Now, we'll take turns in small groups to explore the library area, viewing book bins, furniture, charts, and seating options.

Once you have rotated through each section, turn to a partner and share anything else you are noticing about the classroom library area. Then we'll come back together to think more about the space and hear some of your suggestions.

Closing (1–2 minutes)

So, readers, when it's your day to shop for books in the classroom library during independent reading time, you will find that the books are organized in bins for easy accessibility. After you select books, you'll also notice that there are comfy seating options. So, if you choose to read in this area, be sure to return your seats when you are finished with them. Lastly, should you need a reminder about where to find books or strategies for thinking and talking about books, you'll find the learning charts from our minilessons on the front wall space near the window.

Let's keep talking together about how to make our library space a helpful and comfy space to read, enjoy, talk, think, and connect deeply with books.

A SAMPLE LESSON: MEET THE MATH AREA
Connection/State the Lesson Objective (2–4 minutes)

This year we'll have lots of opportunities to work as mathematicians. To build our math muscles each day, we'll need to get comfortable with taking risks, being brave, asking lots of questions, and making lots of mistakes as we study numbers and math concepts together. To help everyone rise to the challenge, we're going to head over to the back corner of the classroom to tour the space and learn about the resources you will find there. The goal of today's lesson will be to become familiar with this space that is dedicated to our math thinking and problem-solving. OK, let's now head on over to the math space to take a peek at three areas I believe you will find helpful in your work. As long as you can hear and see me, you are welcome to sit, stand, or lean as we gather in the corner.

(Everyone moves from the meeting area to the math area.)

Teach: Guided Inquiry (3–4 minutes)

There are three sections within the space to keep in mind as you explore the area.

First, meet the working space. This area was designed to include all of the resources you need. It is a safe space to collaborate on assignments and to keep track of all of the mathematical thinking we do as a class. The space itself includes a small meeting area, a few unique seating options, and some storage shelves. If you choose to work in this area, you'll have access to the whiteboard table. This is a great place to collaborate on problems using whiteboard tools. There are markers and erasers located under the bench for easy access. There is also a low workbench that also doubles a storage space where you will find additional tools and supplies for upcoming units on money, time, and measurement. Near the math wall, there is a small shelf with a few bins of math read-alouds and puzzles for you to use once you have finished with your daily assignments.

Second, meet the math tools and supply shelf. (I stand in front of the cabinets and remove a container to show a collection of Unifix cubes that are available for use.) The math area was also created to house a variety of tools you can choose from to help you with math tasks and problem-solving. The math tools available to you are located here in the cabinet closest to the back corner of the room. Once you finish using any of the counters, rods, or manipulatives, simply return them to the shelf and container where you found them for others to utilize as well.

You'll also find supplies to assist you in organizing your thinking, including pens, pencils, scratch paper, erasers, small whiteboards, clipboards, graph paper, and extra math notebooks. These items are located on the top two shelves and will help you to visually represent and document your thinking. The bottom shelves hold baskets of our counting collections work. When you finish counting a collection, simply close up the bag and return it to one of these baskets marked for the collections.

Third, meet the math wall. (I walk over to the back-wall space to point out the different aspects of what will be featured.) This wall space will display our collective mathematical thinking. We'll work together to explore concepts, ask questions, pose problems, and investigate a variety of math ideas that will help us grow our understanding. Here we'll build our own landscape of ideas leading toward deeper and more solid conceptual understandings of mathematics. We'll post helpful examples, images, strategies, vocabulary, and symbols to help us keep track of and highlight what we've learned and want to keep in mind across the unit.

Active Engagement (2–4 minutes)

Now I will pass out to each partnership a photo diagram of the space showing a few areas highlighted with boxes and arrows (see Figure 2.18). Go ahead and take a few minutes in your math partnership or trio to first study the image and then share some of your observations, wonder-

ings, and questions you have about the space. I'll be coming around to listen to your discussions, and I will jot down any questions that may come up. Then we'll meet back together to share ideas, suggestions, and some possible answers to your questions with the whole group.

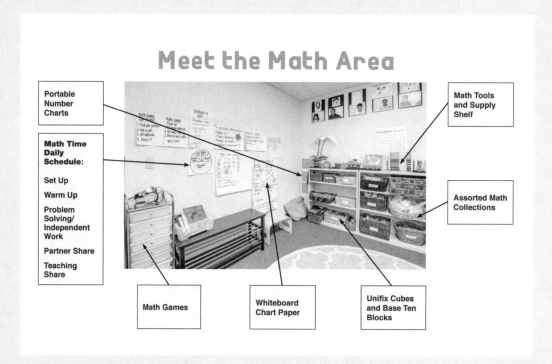

Meet the Math Area

Portable Number Charts

Math Time Daily Schedule:

Set Up

Warm Up

Problem Solving/ Independent Work

Partner Share

Teaching Share

Math Tools and Supply Shelf

Assorted Math Collections

Math Games

Whiteboard Chart Paper

Unifix Cubes and Base Ten Blocks

Figure 2.18

Closing (1–2 minutes)

Everyone will have extended time to explore the space across the week. The purpose of today's lesson was to orientate you to the layout, its purpose, and the resources within it. Should you need a tool to help with a new math challenge, or a reminder about a strategy or how to get started or unstuck, you can find support in this area by utilizing the resources on the math cabinets, collaborating with one another in and around the space, or using the math wall. The math area layout is intended to support your independence and risk-taking in mathematics. Should you have more questions or other ideas about how to improve the space, please let me know by adding your ideas to a sticky note and placing them on our math wall question area. Your feedback is important and will no doubt help everyone.

A QUICK GUIDE TO OTHER SPACES

Learning Space

CLASSROOM LIBRARY

Some Possible Visual Resources

Elements

Area rug

Shelves

Book bins organized in
a variety of ways

Bin for books that are damaged

Pillows

Coffee table

Floor lamp

Flexible seating options

Purpose

A learning space that promotes
- self-selection of reading materials
- independent reading
- partner reading
- book discussion
- research

Participation Opportunities

Explore assortment of books
organized by genre, topic,
author, interest, and series

Find texts of interest

Choose a place to settle in
and read independently

Share, discuss, and debate
ideas with a partner or club

Let a monitor know if a
book is damaged

Some Possible Teaching Ideas

Learning about our classroom library

Knowing when to visit the
library and shop for books

Learning ways to select books

Working independently
in the library space

Returning books to the library

Trying different ways to read
books with my partner

Finding different ways to share
thinking about my reading

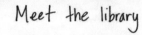

Meet the library

book bins

bookcases

reading spots

book hospital bin

shop

read

share

Using the Library Space

Learning Space
MULTIMEDIA LEARNING SPACES

Elements

Electronic devices

Mobile charging cart

Wi-Fi network

Projector

Tech tools:

- mouse

- speakers

- cables

- adaptors

- clicker

- mounted flat screen

  television or monitor

Flexible seating

Flat-edged table

Portable lap desk

Purpose

To integrate technology into daily teaching and learning opportunities

To nurture authentic learning experiences

To promote innovation

To support online collaboration

To develop digital citizenship skills

To develop global citizenship awareness and skills

Participation Opportunities

Use creativity and productivity apps to differentiate learning

Develop online research skills

Take virtual field trips

Design a digital portfolio

Create:

- podcasts

- apps

- schedules

- surveys

- digital storytelling

Some Possible Teaching Ideas

Introduction to classroom tech tools that can be used in almost any space

Ways to use classroom technology

How to choose tech tools and apps that are applicable

Techniques for making videos on computer screen, aka screen casting

Create classroom resources using QR codes

Basic podcasting tips and strategies

Some Possible Visual Resources

Learning Space

MAKERSPACE, SCIENCE, AND SOCIAL STUDIES SPACE

Elements

Table surface

Storage

Storage containers

Buildable materials:

- cardboard
- scissors
- duct tape
- Legos
- K'nex
- Play-Doh
- modeling clay
- Keva planks
- LED lights
- Snap Circuits

Low-cost and industrial tools

Primary resources

Secondary resources

Purpose

To get curious about the world and materials in it

To create

To imagine

To tinker

To build

To explore the properties of a variety of tools and resources

To nurture higher-level thinking skills

To build problem-solving skills

Participation Opportunities

Build problem-solving skills

Develop flexible learning strategies

Promote interpersonal relationships

Promote critical thinking

Compare and contrast information

Draw connections

Summarize

Develop empathy

Some Possible Teaching Ideas

Explore STEAM concepts

Engage in firsthand experiences with materials and tools

Participate in the design and testing of prototypes

Explore 3D design concepts and fabrication

Learning Space
MATH SUPPLY CENTER

Elements

Shelf or cabinet

Area rug (optional)

Flexible seating

Math supplies:

- assorted blank paper

- graph paper

- writing tools

Math manipulatives:

- counters (Unifix Cubes, blocks, base ten blocks, etc.)

Math tools

- number lines

- number charts

- multiplication chart

Math games

Math read-aloud basket

Purpose

To create a space dedicated to mathematical thinking tools and resources

To display and showcase current student thinking, strategies, and practices

To celebrate and reflect student growth awareness and skills

Participation Opportunities

Retrieve tools/supplies needed for problem-solving tasks

Find examples and resources if I get stuck

Participate in positive ways during math discussions

Some Possible Teaching Ideas

Develop counting strategies

Unpack story problems

Explore sharing protocols

Analyze and discuss number operations

Explore ways to share and debate math thinking with a partner

Develop and practice sentence starters to promote discussion and support the explanation of strategies

Some Possible Visual Resources

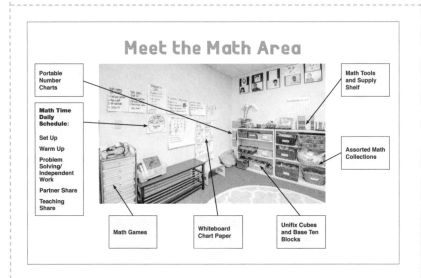

Meet the Math Area

Portable Number Charts

Math Time Daily Schedule:
Set Up
Warm Up
Problem Solving/ Independent Work
Partner Share
Teaching Share

Math Games

Whiteboard Chart Paper

Unifix Cubes and Base Ten Blocks

Math Tools and Supply Shelf

Assorted Math Collections

Care and Maintenance: One way to develop student agency and teach responsibilities is to assign each student or partnership a classroom job or to divide the room up so that a team of students can be responsible for one area or section. Set aside time at the end of each day and at the end of each week to wipe down surfaces and doorknobs, dust shelves, organize materials, clean out bins.

Take photos of classroom areas so there can be a visual guide for what that area should look like. For example, Khalia strategically places photos at eye level so that classroom monitors can't miss them. Once all community members know what the expectations are for keeping the space tidy and organized, the photos can be removed and filed away.

IF–THEN SCENARIOS

If I do not have a budget to update these other spaces in my classroom, then what?

First and foremost, don't feel pressured to use your own money to buy materials or furniture for any areas of your classroom. I know we all spend our own money on our students and classroom, but I really tried to keep track of and limit how much I spent each year. My first suggestion is to decide on what space to update and make a quick sketch. Next, let colleagues know what you are looking for. Sometimes they are eager to give up or trade furniture. Lastly ask (beg, barter, buy a cup of coffee) your plant manager or custodian about what furniture is available on your site, or perhaps call and visit the school district storage and salvage department to learn about the inventory that can be delivered (or picked up) and brought to your classroom.

If those ideas don't work out, there are now many funding streams eager to support educators with classroom needs and learning goals. To develop your own fundraising campaign, visit these crowdfunding sites:

- Donors Choose https://www.donorschoose.org
- Indiegogo https://www.lndiegogo.com
- GoFundMe https://www.gofundme.com
- Fund My Classroom https://www.fundmyclassroom.com
- Class Wishlist https://classwish.org

I feel pretty overwhelmed with all the new technology I'm required to store in my classroom, learn, and use—document camera, SMART Board, laptops, the latest software. I'm having a hard time keeping up with it all and feel way behind my colleagues when it comes to tech. I don't want my students to feel the same way. What's essential and what's not?

First, take a deep breath. Second, try not to put added pressure on yourself. There are steps you can take to reduce anxiety and strong feelings that accompany technology use. The most important, I think, is to find someone that you enjoy being with that could be your tech buddy. Ask them to share their own origin story with technology in the classroom. Make them part of your own personal tech squad when you need encouragement or a reality check. Many of us get started with one tool or application and practice using it over and over again to build familiarity and skill. As with any new skill, time, space, practice, reasonable expectations, and feedback are essential to the learning process. Choose one tech tool or app this upcoming school season and make an effort to use it again and again with your students. You'll likely feel yourself getting more comfortable and confident each time you interact with it.

Second, try to silence the voice of doubt in your head that keeps telling you that you are so far out of the tech loop and there is no way you'll ever catch up to what others are doing. These types of challenges allow us to empathize with the learners in our classrooms who also want to give up on an assignment or project. What would you say to them? How do you rally your learners filled with doubt? I'm guessing something like, "You can do this, and take small steps, or let's go back to a place in your process that you felt good about and build from there." This is a wonderful opportunity to shift your mindset and take some of your own good advice.

Third, adopt a favorite search engine like Google or Yahoo so that when you get stuck or become bewildered you have a protocol in place before you phone a friend. The internet is full of a wide variety of how-to guides, manuals, and YouTube videos on any topic you want to learn more about or problem you encounter. Persistence will be an important quality to practice as you dive into technology. Also, be sure to set up a regular check-in by phone, in person, or Skype with the friend that encouraged and inspired you to get started using technology in the first place. They'll want to hear how your journey is going and no doubt have helpful advice for you each step along the way.

Here are some additional resource links that might be helpful on your journey to becoming more tech-savvy:

- teachersguidetotech.com by Jennifer Gonzalez
- thecornerstoneforteachers.com by Angela Watson
- http://www.spencerauthor.com by John Spencer

If I want to create some additional small-group spaces in my classroom, what are some of the essential ideas I need to keep in mind as I design these spaces for both primary and upper-grade learners?

SAFETY

I'd keep student safety at the top of my list when designing a new space with your learners. Consider how many learners will fit safely in and around it. Be wary of deteriorating furniture and of any exposed flooring, cords, and wires that can cause safety concerns. Consider the purpose of the space and how it will be used. What you are trying to accomplish? How much room do you have?

STUDENT OWNERSHIP

How can you create more opportunities for students to become invested in their work? It's easier than you think: stop making all of the decisions. Make sure that your classroom is adaptable to your students' diverse learning needs. By teaching learners about the purpose of the space, by co-creating the rituals and routines that will govern the space, and by giving learners access to the tools and resources they may need, you help them cultivate their decision-making process to build deeper and more meaningful conceptual understandings of what they are learning about. Learners develop agency and pride in their work when they are invited to take part in the development, organization, and care of the physical classroom space.

ACCESS

How will you level the playing field? The small-group spaces you design with intentionality can change the opportunity structure for your learners. Consider all of the different learning styles and diverse learning needs of your students. Keep in mind that small-group spaces can be equipped with multisensory, multimedia, multilevel, culturally, and linguistically diverse materials. Your learners—no matter the age—will see themselves as competent and capable because of all the opportunistic, inclusive resources you offer.

3

Navigating the Classroom with Flexibility and Ownership

Moving around the classroom is a lot like moving around on the basketball court. Players, like students, navigate most effectively once they become familiar with the space and learn to pay attention to one another. On the basketball court, movement and spacing is often dictated by the defense. Defenders are careful not to move too close to the opposing player for fear of becoming the victim of the dreaded crossover dribble or a wide-open jump shot. Generally, you achieve a more strategic level of play and higher winning percentage when you pay attention to the court parameters and have a healthy respect for your opponent and fellow teammates.

In the classroom, space and movement work in similar ways. Students, like players, learn how to carefully navigate around objects (in this case, furniture) and each other's "bubbles of space." When learners are intentional and purposeful with their movements, this effort typically results in better performance and higher rates of task completion. On the other hand, when learners move around the classroom aimlessly, or seemingly in a rush, these efforts tend to lead to disruptive behaviors, which often result in the loss of instructional and independent

When students have choice, they gain control over their learning. When they are given choices of where to sit, they feel more competent to choose what is best for them to enhance their learning. It helps them become more involved with their learning because they are the ones who are making decisions regarding their environment and their order of completing tasks.

—CHARLOTTE DANIELSON,
THE FRAMEWORK FOR TEACHING: EVALUATION INSTRUMENT

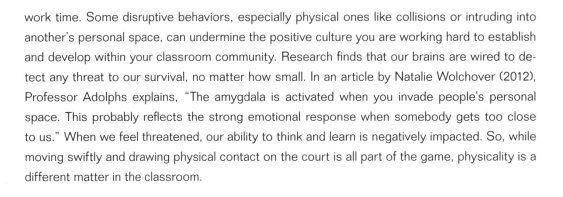

work time. Some disruptive behaviors, especially physical ones like collisions or intruding into another's personal space, can undermine the positive culture you are working hard to establish and develop within your classroom community. Research finds that our brains are wired to detect any threat to our survival, no matter how small. In an article by Natalie Wolchover (2012), Professor Adolphs explains, "The amygdala is activated when you invade people's personal space. This probably reflects the strong emotional response when somebody gets too close to us." When we feel threatened, our ability to think and learn is negatively impacted. So, while moving swiftly and drawing physical contact on the court is all part of the game, physicality is a different matter in the classroom.

Co-Authoring Expectations Around Moving and Learning

Movement is essential to learning. Research on the benefits of movement are overwhelmingly positive and support a correlation between levels of activity, physical fitness, and cognitive ability among young learners (Sibley and Etnier 2003). Educators that have found ways to incorporate movement between lessons and into their teaching and learning experiences have noted increases in student engagement, focus, and attention, and a decrease in disruptive behaviors (Wilson 2014). When we invest the time to think and talk about how to move around the classroom with care and efficiency, we create a culture of compassion and connectedness. It's essential to join together as a learning community to coauthor expectations around moving and learning together. According to the founder of Reggio Emilia's educational philosophy, Loris Malaguzzi, "It was not so much that we need to think of the child who develops himself by himself but rather of a child who develops himself interacting and developing with others" (Rankin 2004, 82). Setting aside regular opportunities for students to meet and discuss what it feels like to move and work inside of the classroom is an important protocol. Everyone's expectations about how to move and work efficiently will surely grow and change across the school year as the community builds more stamina for learning and gets to know each other better. For example, in autumn, common opening rituals and routines like entering the classroom or gathering in the whole-group space will likely feel clumsy and slow until learners become familiar with the areas and pathways and work together to navigate them. This is the perfect time to observe and point out what's working well, chart it, and to encourage learners to keep doing what is working—perhaps even making it better. It's also the ideal time to work with students as design partners and to get feedback on things that seem confusing and/or may not be going well as they move around the classroom at different intervals. While you have everyone's attention, discuss ways to determine which challenges feel the hardest and collect theories about why. Work together during a "solution session" to chart creative ideas and options that may include rearranging the physical environment. Once everyone agrees to a few viable options, provide lots of opportunities to practice and reflect back on their effectiveness.

Setting Up Ground Rules for Movement

Just as basketball players equip themselves with the proper clothes, shoes, gear, and a game plan that allows them to work together on the court, so too must learners come prepared for tasks with the proper tools, a plan of action, and a purpose for their learning in the classroom. Start by establishing some ground rules for you and your students to follow so they can actively participate in positive ways. Here are a few examples to consider:

1. Establish a structure that allows for all voices to be heard. Consider a variety of ways learners can give feedback about how movement in the classroom is going, including verbal, written, pictorial, and digital.

2. Always include the option to "pass" during classroom discussions without shame or judgment.

3. Demonstrate, rehearse, and practice any procedures or protocols that are agreed upon.

4. Develop questions together with the purpose of promoting active participation and documenting collective thinking. Chart responses. A few examples of questions might be

   • What are some of the expectations you have of each other and of the teacher when it comes to moving around the classroom?

   • What are some ways we can move around the classroom without disturbing others while they are working?

   • How might we move around classmates that might be in our way?

   • How might we describe our movement routines to a new student?

   • What tools or resources might we need to help us move around the classroom more efficiently?

5. Conduct a movement assessment (like the one in Figure 3.1) and create an action plan based on what you learn. With your learners, list what's been working well and where there are opportunities for growth.

Figure 3.1 Movement Assessment

Movement Assessment

Type of Movement	Working Well	Opportunities for Growth
Arriving to the classroom	When we arrive, there is time to greet the teacher and our friends before starting the day. Putting our backpacks away on hooks before coming into the classroom leaves more space in the room to work. Sitting where we want is fun.	Sometimes it's hard to move past students in other classrooms to get to our line in the morning. It's too loud as people walk in the classroom (chatting, talking, eating). Too cluttered to walk down aisles because some people bring in their backpacks instead of using the hooks outside. First come, first served rule about where to sit. It feels annoying and unfair.
Departing the classroom	Everyone has a cleanup zone so that helps a lot with cleanup at the end of the day. We end our day all together in a brief community circle.	Sometimes it feels squished coming in and out of the classroom at the end of the day. It's because • folks are not paying attention • there are people in the way Sometimes students cut the line to get out of classroom more quickly. It gets really loud and noisy as we are trying to pack up and leave the classroom.
Movement *during* learning block	After the whole-group lesson, we can move around to find another space if the first one we chose is not working. There are lots of work spaces to choose from: • seven table pods • classroom library • rug area • back classroom corners If we have a question or need to check in with a partner, we do not have to raise our hand.	Some students are taking shortcuts around work spaces to get to the supply center more quickly—bumping chairs.

Movement *between* two learning blocks

Supplies organized in different areas is helpful. Math supplies, art supplies, and writing supplies all have specific shelves so that makes walking around the room to find things go more smoothly.

Sometimes there is not enough time to clean up, put away supplies, and get ready for the next part of the day.

Sometimes during group activities, classmates begin to work before everyone is set up and ready to start.

It gets loud when we try to put away and gather supplies, then move from one work space to the next one.

Using the list of opportunities for growth, identify some things you'd like to work on as a class. Choose one growth opportunity at a time and look for any patterns or recurring concerns. In Figure 3.1 the highlighted sentences show that loudness is a recurring issue, so we decided to work on that. We had to ask ourselves: What changes do we agree to make to work on noise level? Figure 3.2 shows the Movement Action Plan we drafted.

Figure 3.2 Draft of Movement Action Plan

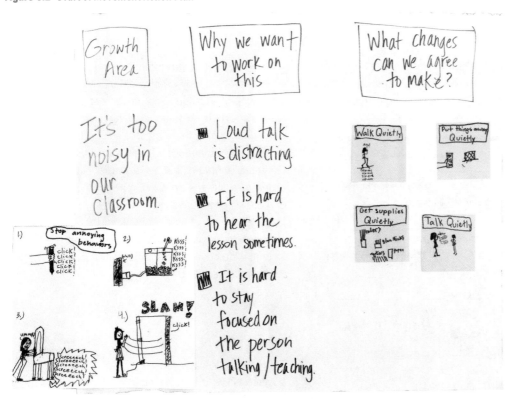

I typed up the Movement Action Plan, as shown in Figure 3.3, so students could access it in different ways.

Figure 3.3 Movement Action Plan

Movement Action Plan

Growth Area	Why Do We Want to Work on This?	What Changes Can We Make?
It's too noisy in our classroom.	It's hard to stay focused when the room is noisy. Loud talking is distracting. It's hard to hear the small-group lesson with the teacher.	Pay more attention to the noises our bodies make when we move around the classroom: • stomping around • shuffling feet • putting things down harshly • handling supplies carelessly Stop annoying behaviors and avoid sharp, sudden movements that sometimes cause confusion, stress, and outbursts: • getting up to sharpen pencils • clicking pens • dragging chairs

Figure 3.4 Individualized Movement Plan: Sticky Note

Figure 3.5 Individualized Movement Plan: Checklist

Figure 3.6 Individualized Movement Plan: Graphic Organizer

6. Create individualized movement plans. When you set up ground rules for movement, you'll probably notice that some students may need additional support. Consider working with each student to develop an individualized movement plan. Use whatever tool they think might work best to help them reach a self-created movement goal. To get started, try using sticky notes, checklists, or graphic organizers, like the ones in Figures 3.4, 3.5, and 3.6. These individualized plans were first kept on top of student work folders. As independence grew, the artifacts moved to the inside cover of the folder until they were no longer needed.

Accessing Supplies with Purpose

Former UCLA basketball legendary coach John Wooden started the very first practice of each season with a lesson on how to tie shoes and put on socks properly to prevent blisters and ankle sprains. It was a surprise first lesson for the rookie class. Coach Wooden knew that the proper care and preparation of a player's most basic tools, in this case shoes and socks, would allow a player to focus on the bigger tasks at hand. "Failing to prepare is preparing to fail" was one of his famous mantras. So how do we prepare our students to access supplies and materials, so they can focus on the bigger tasks at hand and move with purpose? (See Figures 3.7–3.11.)

1. Develop, explain, and practice supply retrieval protocols together. To prevent traffic jams, teach students to move clockwise in supply areas.

2. Make sure classroom supplies and materials are both centrally located and within arm's reach. Place a few small pencil or pen storage caddies around the classroom. This will eliminate the need to walk all the way across a room to find a sharpened pencil or make a paper choice. You might even consider marking the pencils so that learners know which caddie to return it to if they forget.

3. Relocate or downsize supply area locations if they are counterproductive.

4. Leave supply containers open at the top and labeled on the side. This makes for easier returns when learners are dropping off supplies. Also, go ahead and store tops of bins inside a closet for easy end of the year storage. You can just pop the tops back on and stack them in your closet.

5. Assign monitors to pass out, pick up, and deliver supplies to small-group work areas. This will help to alleviate traffic jams during both pre- and post-independent work time.

6. Assign monitors to organize supplies and to let you know when it is time to replenish supplies.

7. Teach students to use resources sparingly, taking only what they need.

8. Share with students that your supply budget is finite and make decisions together about what to purchase. This is real-world math problem-solving.

Part of being prepared is also having the time to practice. Carve out time for students to rehearse supply retrieval using different pathways. Remind them to steadily move in the clockwise direction when at supply stations. Offer different scenarios and configurations: partners make a trip to the math supply station to gather a bin of base ten blocks to solve a multiplication story problem; an impatient writer stops by a busy writing supply area and wants to quickly pick up a

Figures 3.7a, 3.7b, 3.7c, 3.7d
Kindergarten classroom. Rosanne's kindergarten classroom was smaller than most, so she coached her students to prevent traffic jams by entering and exiting the library area in a clockwise direction when returning materials like books and reading supplies (baggies, bookmarks, reading glasses). Notice how the girls cleaned the space they were working in, returned supplies to the shelf, and then joined the class in its whole-group meeting area.

Figures 3.8a, 3.8b, 3.8c, 3.8d, 3.8e
First-grade classroom. Dibanhi selected a collection from the assorted bin, then chose to practice counting on the rug in the library area. Once she counted to fifty, she realized she needed a math tool to keep going with her counting. She headed over to the math supply station to pick up a math toolkit, selected a number chart, and then resumed her work using the chart to help her keep track as she counted. A little later, the teacher and a few classmates came over to see what she was working on and to join the counting. Shayla took notes on the collective math thinking and reasoning that was happening as Dibanhi shared her process of counting objects past fifty.

81

Figure 3.9 Third-grade classroom. When Anthony arrived in the morning, he retrieved his independent reading tools from a two-way cubby. To prevent traffic jams at the supply center, Jamaica decided to keep supply station shelving away from walls, so learners could access supplies no matter what direction they were coming from.

Figures 3.10a, 3.10b, 3.10c Fourth-grade classroom. In between lessons, students were invited to move from their assigned home base seat to a self-selected writing spot. Raenah, for example, gathered study materials, pushed in her chair, and perched herself atop a shelf that also served as a seating option near a window. This was one of her favorite individual work spaces in the classroom.

Figures 3.11a, 3.11b, 3.11c Third-grade classroom. Students are encouraged to move in and out of their independent work areas to gather needed supplies without asking for permission. Sitting off to the side, Evelyn listened in on a writing conference happening at a nearby table. Overhearing a strategy that she also wanted to try, she quickly visited a nearby writing supply station to pick up some revision tools and then headed back to her spot to continue working on her own.

revision pen after having a writing conference with a teacher; or a small group of learners takes a quick visit to the inquiry table to look through and select a primary resource to use with an ongoing collaborative project. The point of practicing different scenarios is to make sure learners know where to find tools and how to acquire them efficiently, without wasting time or asking for permission. Attempt to store everyday materials and supplies in places where they are easily visible and accessible to students rather than behind closet doors or inside file cabinets (Olson and Platt 2000). Creating a culture of intentional movement to get needed supplies before, during, or after an independent work period develops agency, fosters trust, and celebrates a proactive stance toward preparation for learning.

Making Transitions Run Smoothly

We all want learners to feel successful at navigating the classroom as they make transitions—to get started on the school day or task, pack up at the end of the day, or move from one task to another. To make transitions run more smoothly, we'll need to plan and help learners use the classroom space to meet their social and academic goals. Famed entrepreneur, philanthropist,

Figures 3.12a, 3.12b, 3.12c Fourth-grade classroom. Arrival routines in Lori's classroom included unpacking personal supplies on hooks outside of the classroom, turning in homework, and taking down chairs before starting the day with independent reading time.

Figures 3.13a and 3.13b Fourth-grade classroom. Students need lots of practice to be able to move efficiently in or out of a classroom's whole-group space. Before departing a math lesson, Lori often asked her learners to take a moment to envision a plan for the work they would strive to accomplish that day. Providing additional think time before leaving the whole-group space will stagger departure times and help to alleviate traffic jams.

Figures 3.14a and 3.14b Fourth-grade classroom. Finding inclusive ways to accommodate learners' classroom-movement needs is important. Kody joined the whole-group discussion then decided to return briefly to his desk to gather his notebook so that he could record some key information from the lesson. Knowing Kody well, Lori invited him to sit in a strategic spot that allowed him to get up and move easily without disturbing others.

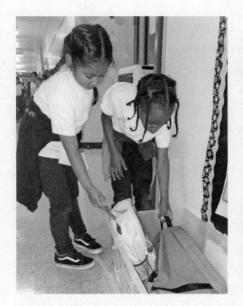

Figures 3.15a and 3.15b
First-grade classroom. In Shayla's classroom, Montrail and Dibanhi gathered their personal belongings from a bin just outside of the doorway, then stopped by the homework cubby to pick up their take-home assignment before joining classmates in the meeting area to say goodbye.

◀ ◀ **Figures 3.16a and 3.16b**
Fourth-grade classroom. Departure routines in Lori's classroom included staggered times to retrieve backpacks and homework folders, jotting down assignments, and finding a buddy to depart the room with once the school day was over.

and life coach Tony Robbins writes a lot about goals and how to realistically meet them. Robbins offers, "you need a vision that's large, and you need a plan that's achievable" (Friedlander 2018). Often both educators and students give up on their plans too quickly into the school year. We don't realize that success is really about the growth process happening within us over time while we work to try and achieve a goal. "Success is growth," says Robbins (Friedlander 2018). So, what can we do to support students with successfully knowing and implementing the expectations of participation when it comes to making efficient classroom transitions? First, be clear what the expectations for behaviors are during transition times. Give students a chance to give you feedback on these expectations if you have not co-authored them together. Learners should have ample think time to process where they are going, what they'll be doing, what they'll need to bring, how to get there, and how long it should realistically take to settle in. Imagine for yourself how much better your own life transitions might go if you took the time to make a plan for how you would move throughout your day. (See Figures 3.12–3.16.)

Second, after giving a few opportunities to rehearse transitions and observe participation behaviors, spend time revising any agreements and expectations that need clarification, and celebrate the positive aspects of what they have accomplished within a measured timeframe. Chart what you learn. Your chart may include some of the transitions and tasks in Figure 3.17.

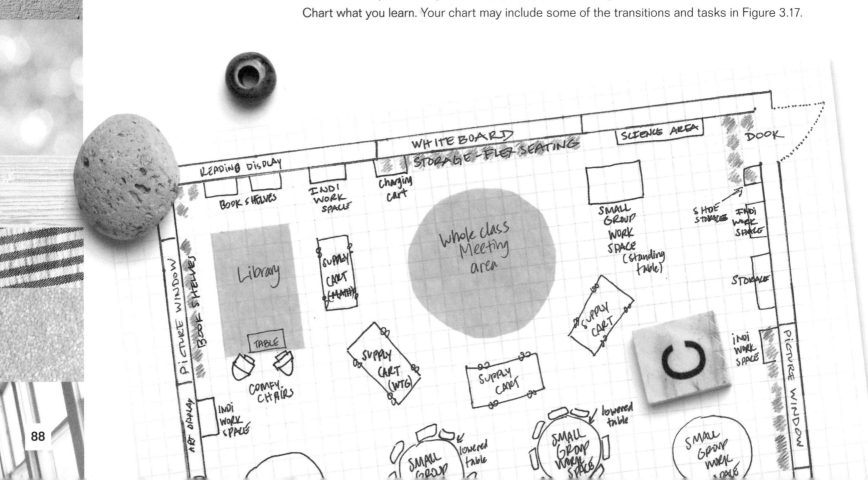

Figure 3.17 Establishing Agreements for Movement

Establishing Agreements for Movement
(Co-Authored with Students)

Transition	Expectation	Examples of Rituals and Routines That Help Us Meet Expectations	How Will We Know We Did It?
Entering the classroom	Learners prepare for the start of the day by consistently attending to morning routines and rituals with independence.	Make eye contact. Say hello and good morning. Shake hands (if it's flu season, try fist bumps, elbow taps, or air high-fives). Put away personal belongings, either on shelves, on hooks, or in cubbies. Carefully move stacked chairs from the top of the desk to the floor. Find a work space to get started on a self-selected activity. Complete your classroom job or morning responsibility (feed pet, water plants, turn on lamps, etc.). Take attendance (assign a student attendance monitor or use a magnetic board, pocket chart, or digital device). Begin the day with a variety of warm-up tasks. Prepare for the day by reviewing notes and assignments from the prior class meeting.	Everyone feels seen, ready, and connected to their peers, the teacher(s), and the environment when they start the day. (Use a student attitude survey to document results.) The classroom is alive and busy with everyone moving around taking care of their morning business instead of being silly or playing around.
Exiting the classroom	Learners prepare for the close of the day by immediately executing closing routines and rituals with reverence and independence all the time.	Jot down any notes or homework assignments. Check in with your partner or table team about any accountability tasks. Perform your classroom job or responsibility. Put up the chairs. Tidy up your classroom area. Participate in goodbye rituals (song, chant, rap, reflections, celebrations, etc.).	Everyone helps with the end-of-the-day tasks instead of only a few students doing all the cleanup. There is time for learners to come together for a few minutes to close the day or session as a community.

Establishing Agreements for Movement
(Co-Authored with Students) cont.

Transition	Expectation	Examples of Rituals and Routines That Help Us Meet Expectations	How Will We Know We Did It?
Moving from one curricular area to another in the same classroom	Learners are organized and transition to new tasks and work spaces with peers or on their own.	Clean up your space. Return materials to their proper place(s). Put away and gather materials for the next activity. Move to the next space.	Everyone is quick to set up for their own learning, then works to make sure others are ready too.
Moving during a classroom activity	Learners are proactive about asking for help and getting supplies to complete a project, assignment, or task.	Follow classroom protocol for bathroom use. Find help with a peer after trying on your own to problem-solve issues that arise. Walk quietly to supply areas or shelves to retrieve any additional tools or supplies.	Everyone assumes the identity of resourceful problem solvers—knowing what they need and where to go, versus waiting or walking aimlessly around the classroom looking for help.
Moving in other spaces in the school	Learners transfer the same behaviors used for movement in the classroom to other learning spaces on campus.	Clean up space. Drop off materials to cubby and pick up new supplies for new task. Find a spot in new classroom space. Set up work space and begin work.	The school leadership, librarian, games coach, and music teacher give us feedback that our classroom community moves through campus spaces in respectful ways.

When Movement Breaks Down

Breakdowns happen. Movement on the court and in the classroom tends to break down for a variety or combination of reasons. During a basketball game, if the opposing team intercepts the ball and runs down the court to execute an alley-oop, a defensive breakdown has occurred. This usually happens as a result of a miscommunication between players or just plain being outhustled. The same way we can anticipate challenges with movement on the basketball court, we can forecast challenges with movement in our classroom. Being able to avoid breakdowns before they happen is the simplest solution. Think about the parts of the day when movement in the classroom becomes the most problematic for learners and leads to loss of time, productivity, energy, and focus, and negative interactions between students. Let's begin to imagine what strategies we can offer learners to decrease breakdowns with regard to movement in the classroom. Begin to develop student awareness of the potential risks of entering an overcrowded area. Teach learners how to anticipate outcomes based on the information they are receiving with their senses. Invite them to take on more responsibility for their thoughts, words, and actions when moving in the classroom. Having conversations early and often during community meetings will yield more empathetic, positive, and productive outcomes for the entire community.

Breakdowns in movement most often occur when large groups of students are moving at the same time into or out of the same area. Let's call these traffic jams. For example, when students are entering and exiting the classroom, whole-group meeting area, and supply stations at the same time, movement becomes tight, even restricted, which can lead to off-task and disruptive behaviors that take time away from productivity.

"Research reveals that effective teachers differentiate; develop clear goals for student learning and link classroom activities to them; make the most of instructional time through smooth transitions and limited disruptions; and create situations in which students can succeed and feel safe in taking academic risks" (Stronge and Hindman 2003, 49). Figure 3.18 is a chart of some of the most common breakdowns that occur when students are moving in and around the classroom. It also offers some possible strategies for students within a variety of settings to prevent these challenges from happening in the first place.

Figure 3.18 Common Movement Breakdowns, Strategies, and Visual Support

Common Breakdowns	Some Proactive Strategies	Some Possible Visual Support Tools for Learners
Entering and exiting the classroom	When possible, avoid lining up near the doorway by teaching learners to • unpack and store personal belongings on or in hooks, bins, or cubbies prior to entering the classroom • enter the classroom as they arrive and begin/end the day or period with a "soft-start" or "soft-closing" (independent reading or a choice activity that does not include extensive preparation) • stagger their entry in and out of doorways via preassigned teams of partnerships, trios, or quads	
Entering and exiting the whole-group meeting area.	Rally learners to • utilize different pathways leading in and out of the meeting area • move in a clockwise direction when entering or exiting the meeting area • move into and out of the meeting area as teams, tablemates, or project groups	
Accessing and returning supplies	Encourage learners to move in a clockwise direction as they approach the supply station. Move supply stations away from the wall to create easy-access points from any direction. Create mini supply stations around the room to avoid congestion. Invite learners to take only what they need. They can return to gather additional supplies, as needed. Organize supplies into labeled containers so that it will be faster and easier for learners to find materials the next time they need them.	

When it's time to move about the classroom between lessons, preparing students to move in certain ways when they hear and/or see a few calming cues can foster ownership and independence during times when we need everyone to get started on their work and move together in harmony. "Efficient and smooth transitions will provide teachers with more instructional time. Moreover, planned transitions can also be learning situations for children, emphasizing connections and relationships of activities and thoughts," (Vartuli and Phelps 1980, 94).

Support students with movement around the classroom by trying out a variety of methods like the examples in Figure 3.19. Get feedback from students about which ones are the most helpful and work best for them.

Figure 3.19 A Few Samples of Visual Reminders to Support Movement

Verbal and Nonverbal Cues	What Learners Could Do	Visual Support
Music	Stop and take a deep breath. Ground yourself in your seat. Move slowly to put away work and supplies. Return to meeting area before music ends.	
Hand up.	Come to a good stopping point with your thinking partner. Stop and take a deep breath. Get your mind and body ready to rejoin the whole-group discussion or lesson.	
On a whiteboard, screenshot an image that denotes it's time to make a transition. Displaying a large digital timer is also helpful.	Notice the image or screenshot depicting the end of the day's rituals. Collaborate with peers to tidy up the classroom. Gather your personal belongings. Return to your seat or meeting area.	

Teaching into Movement

When we take some time to delve into *how* we will move around the classroom, it supports *why* we are doing this work. Craft procedures and language together with students to create buy-in. It is important for learners to have cognitive clarity when they are acquiring new knowledge. Make sure to explain why this work is important to the classroom community. Here's a lesson about moving between two work areas in our classroom, using the architecture of minilessons defined by the Teachers College Reading and Writing Project (Calkins 2003).

A SAMPLE LESSON: MAKING SMOOTH MOVES WITHIN THE CLASSROOM (PART ONE)

Connection (1–2 minutes)

There are a lot of us in this small space and we are getting good at sharing supplies, tools, furniture, and ideas. Taking care of one another and our resources is essential to a happy and productive learning community. Another way we can show care for one another is to be mindful of how we move our bodies in and around the classroom as we strive to get work done. A few classmates have asked me to talk about being safer around the classroom. Yesterday I studied how we exit and enter our meeting area. I also observed how we journey from one small-group work area to another. I am wondering if any of you think that we could be more mindful of our bodies as we move around the classroom. What if we paid more attention to our arms, hands, and feet as we moved around the classroom? Paying closer attention to our bodies as we pass one another and walk around the room may address the safety concerns that are coming up. I'd like to share with you an idea I had about moving around the classroom safely and efficiently.

Teach: Guided Inquiry (5–7 minutes)

Let's play some games that will help everyone use what I call smooth moves in and around our classroom. Have you heard of smooth moves? To be smooth, you've got to talk smooth. You've got to think smooth. I am now going to pass out marbles so that you all can feel something smooth. Let's also play a game. It's called Thumbs Up, Thumbs Down. I will call out the names of a few items and you will give a thumbs up for items that you think feel smooth and thumbs down for items that feel rough. Ready? Sandpaper? River stones? Butterfly wings? Tree bark? Glass? Grater? Great. So, items that are smooth are river stones, butterfly wings, and glass. OK, so now let's think about defining the word smooth as a word that all of these items have in common. Take a minute with a partner to try and say what you think the word smooth means. (Listen in to capture a few partnership responses from the rug and write them down on the whiteboard.)

Let's all meet back together and discuss a possible definition for the word smooth. We've gathered descriptions: flat surface, even all around, without any bumps, and no hard edges. Does this work for our definition? Yes? (The community agrees.) OK, let's go with it for now and then we can revise the definition if we need to.

Now that you know what I mean by smooth, *let's play another game and think together about what smooth moves might look like with our bodies. I have a few sticky notes with some moves written down on them. I am going to call up a few classmates to act out these scenarios while displaying either smooth or rough moves. Let's continue with making it interactive by giving each scenario a thumbs up for a smooth move and a thumbs down for rough. Got it? Ready? (Randomly choose a few students to demonstrate the moves on the sticky notes in front of the class. Getting the whole body involved helps transfer the concept of smooth into a way of being, and it's a way to positively participate in the classroom. These are some of the possible scenarios for your sticky notes:*

- Skipping into the classroom with your hands cheering
- Walking with your hands down and to the side on the way to lunch
- Tossing a book into a library bin
- Walking backwards to the whole-group meeting area
- Standing up, pushing your chair in, and returning items to the writing center
- Using two hands to carefully lift art materials from the art supply shelf)

Closing (1–2 minutes)

I hope that both of those games help us understand what it means to move smoothly, evenly, and without bumps around the classroom. Tomorrow we'll work on how we can incorporate smooth moves into parts of our day. Moving smoothly from one task or project to the next is about having a plan in mind.

A SAMPLE LESSON: MAKING SMOOTH MOVES WITHIN THE CLASSROOM (PART TWO)

Connection (1–2 minutes)

*Let's continue with our work from yesterday. We did a bit of inquiry about things that are smooth and rough. Then we created our own definition of the word **smooth**. Afterward, we played a game that got us thinking about our body awareness and how to move smoothly and thoughtfully into and out of spaces. Today I'd like to show you how having a plan helps me focus on what I need to get done as well as how I get it done.*

Teach: Demonstration Lesson (3–5 minutes)

A four-step plan that helps me move smoothly through my day typically goes like this:

1. *Think about a task or project.*

2. *Use smooth moves to gather supplies.*

3. *Use smooth moves to find a work spot.*

4. *Use smooth moves to get started and to finish.*

(Once you chart your plan of action with your students, demonstrate it right away in real time so that they see an example of how things might go.)

Watch me use smooth moves as I plan to work on my project. First, I will reread my plan to help me think about the steps I will take. Next, I will stop and think about what I want to work on. I close my eyes and remember that I did not finish a writing entry in my science log. (Go ahead and continue to read all four steps out loud, naming each step and the smooth moves you will make.)

I take notes to prepare my moves ahead of time. It might look something like this:

1. Think about a task or project (Quietly stand or sit and think. Close eyes and picture the task.).

2. Use smooth moves to gather supplies (Walk slowly to the supply area. Wait patiently for the person ahead of you to choose supplies. Collect your personal supplies. Open and close doors and drawers.).

3. Use smooth moves to find a work spot (Tour the classroom space. Choose a seating option.).

4. Use smooth moves to get started and to finish (Focus on your breathing while you settle into your work space. Organize supplies on a nearby work surface. Get up slowly. Return items into their baskets.).

Active Engagement (2–4 minutes)

Now it's your turn. With a plan in mind, you're going to practice moving smoothly around the classroom. Here is your scenario. Often before our writing lesson begins, we get set up for writing by gathering our supplies and finding a writing spot. Go ahead and start making a plan in your mind for getting set up for writing. Next, get a picture in your mind of what you will need to gather from your desk and the writing supply center to help you accomplish your writing goal. You can use your fingers to think through the steps if it helps. Then, when you are ready, stand up, look around, and take a few seconds to think about the direction you will take to carefully and smoothly gather any materials you need. Once you have your supplies, choose an area and get started on your work. I will call everyone back together once the room is set up to see how your plan went and to talk about any challenges that came up. OK, head out and get set up for writing time.

(After students find a space to begin work, invite them back to the meeting area.)

Writers, leave your supplies in your spot and let's quickly meet back together in our whole-group space for a few minutes to reflect on how your plan went while moving to your writing spot. Let's have you and your thought partner take two minutes to turn and talk about the smooth moves you made. What are some of your ideas about how it could go more smoothly? (Share.)

Our next step is to think about some of the challenges we faced when we tried to move efficiently and respectfully around the classroom to gather materials, find a spot, and start to work. Let's name and chart the hard parts and then come up with some ideas about how we can handle these scenarios in respectful ways.

(Use a whiteboard or chart paper to make a list after students have had a chance to brainstorm with a partner. For emergent bilinguals and emergent readers, include photos or illustrations as visual examples. See Figure 3.26.)

Figure 3.20 Smooth Moves

SMOOTH MOVES: CHALLENGES AND SOLUTIONS

Challenges	Possible Solutions
Someone standing in the way	- Wait. - Say "excuse me." - Say "excuse me" again but louder (if they didn't hear you the first time).
Furniture in the way	- Move the furniture. - Return furniture (push in chair or return flexible seating option to its storage area).
Someone choosing the same spot	- Go ahead and choose another spot; it's not a big deal. - Ask nicely to "please move over." - Ask nicely to "please choose another spot." - Remind them in a kind voice to look at the seating map, if spots are assigned.
Someone bumping into me	- Let them know how it made you feel by using an "I" statement. ("I didn't like it when . . ."). - If they apologize, consider accepting their apology. - If they don't apologize, and you feel like they should, ask for an apology or ask for help.
Traffic jams	- Slow down and wait your turn. - Try moving to another side that gives you better access. - After waiting a few minutes, return to gather supplies.

Closing (1–2 minutes)

Pick one thing that you will work on. Tell your thought partner what it is. As a community that cares about one another and enjoys working together, it will be important to take the time to think about and plan out how to move around the classroom smoothly. From now on, let's all be sure to practice making smooth moves as we enter and exit the classroom and as we move to and from different work areas. If we run into any challenges, we can refer to the chart for help.

A QUICK GUIDE TO MOVEMENT

Type of Movement

ARRIVING AND ENTERING THE CLASSROOM AT THE START OF THE DAY

Anchor Charts/Visual Resources That Support Learners

Possible Goals

To calm any anxieties related to the home-to-school transition

To support students with preparation and organization work

To promote a sense of belonging in the community

Elements

Students
Backpack and personal gear

A variety of storage options:
- hooks
- cubbies
- containers/baskets

A self-check-in tool for attendance:
- clipboard
- whiteboard
- electronic device

A variety of classroom "thinking" tools and supplies

What It Might Look Like

Students
Storing or hanging up backpacks and personal gear

Making eye contact with one another

Turning in assignments to the central location

Self-selecting a morning activity

Gathering in the whole-group space to start the day together

Meeting with a partner

Meeting with the teacher

What It Might Sound Like

Students
Greeting each other and the teacher

Stowing gear

Asking follow-up questions to partners and teacher about projects and/assignments

Collecting supplies and project materials

Discussing goals and project check-in work in small groups

Some Possible Lesson Ideas

Ways to greet others

Ways to stow personal gear

Homework turn-in protocols

How to self-select a start of the day activity

How to log independent reading/writing time

 SET UP MATH
Get your * cubby

 Find a * comfy spot near partner
start working on ... not done
work in red folder

 Set Up - Writing
GET your * cubby and pen

 FIND a * comfy spot
· personal space

 start working on ...not done
stories in blue folder

 Set Up - Rotations
Get your * cubby

 Find a * Comfy Spot
· personal space

 start * Read to Self Time

Type of Movement

MOVING INTO/OUT OF CLASSROOM (FOR LUNCH, RECESS, OTHER CLASSES)

Possible Goals

To transition with independence into and out of the classroom during breaks in the day

To develop agency

To practice problem-solving skills

To cultivate agility

Elements

Students
A variety of classroom "thinking" tools and supplies

Students and Teacher
Charts with words, phrases, photos, and/or images that show examples of co-authored and agreed upon ways to move around the classroom

What It Might Look Like

Students
Reentering and exiting the classroom in ways that avoid collision and unnecessary contact

Making decisions about the best pathways to use upon reentering the classroom

Gathering "thinking" tools and supplies

Selecting flexible seating options with possible distractions in mind

What It Might Sound Like

Students
Using whisper voices when talking with peers and teacher

Moving to perimeter areas of the classroom for side conversations in lowered voices

Some Possible Lesson Ideas

Ways to enter and exit the classroom:

- using traditional one/two lines

- establishing a line order

- deciding on a partner, group, or team order

- inviting an open line-up ritual

Ways to differentiate experiences for learners who may need additional time transitioning in/out of the classroom

Type of Movement

MOVING AROUND THE ROOM

Possible Goals

To flexibly move from one physical learning space to another (and vice versa):

- whole to small

- whole to individual

- small to small

- small to individual

- small to whole

To transition from one classroom activity to the next without losing focus, train of thought, or becoming distracted

To quickly retrieve and return materials to a supply area

Elements

Students
A variety of classroom "thinking" tools and supplies (paper, pens, etc.)

Flexible seating options

What It Might Look Like

Students
Walking slowly with intention from one area to the next

Retrieving "thinking" tools and supplies, as needed, from different areas of the classroom

Selecting flexible seating options

Collaborating with peers on projects

Preparing to meet with teacher 1:1 or in a small group

What It Might Sound Like

Students
Planning how to go about accomplishing a task

Discussing which supplies are the best tools for a task

Negotiating work area choices and flexible seating options

Asking questions for clarity about assignments with partners

Reminding others about movement procedures

Some Possible Lesson Ideas

How to respectfully move around someone or something that is in your way

What to do when you think you are done

What to do when you don't have and/or can't find the supplies you need

Ideas for when group or partner collaboration and/or conversations break down

Routines for cleaning up classroom areas

Type of Movement

DEPARTING THE CLASSROOM
AT THE END OF THE DAY

Possible Goals

To depart the day with co-authored and agreed upon community closing rituals

To return and organize all classroom tools, resources, and supplies to their established location

Elements

Students

Classroom job chart or upkeep schedule

School event calendar

Student cubbies or filing system (box/cabinet/shelf)

Charted schedule, poem, verse, or text for closing ritual

What It Might Look Like

Students

Using the classroom job chart to determine upkeep schedule

Assisting peers with classroom tidying-up routines

Returning tools and resources to their designated supply areas

Passing out assignments

Participating in closing/goodbye rituals

What It Might Sound Like

Students

Reminding peers about classroom responsibilities for tidying up

Checking about assignments and due dates

Making public affirmations, acknowledgments of thanks, and apologies

Sharing of a song, game, closing verse, or activity (read-aloud)

Some Possible Lesson Ideas

Ways we want to close our day/period together

Tidy-up tips for organizing classroom areas before exiting the classroom

Ways to handle "hard to clean up" areas

What to do when peers won't help with their part of a classroom job responsibility

IF-THEN SCENARIOS

If I let students get up and move whenever they want to, then how will I be able to control and maintain a calm working environment where everyone can complete their assignments without distractions?

Let's first start with the idea of a "calm working environment." Calm is relative. How will you and your learners redefine calm? Student engagement and effort levels rise and fall throughout the day. What will make the difference in your work environment? Most likely patience, planning, classroom community discussions, consistency, and praise over time. Teaching students how to move around and collaborate in a classroom space requires lots of practice and do-overs.

You will need to model patience with your thoughts, words, and actions. Be sure to also recruit and then support student leaders to take the lead on moving efficiently around the classroom in calm ways and encouraging their peers to work and move in the same calm, intentional, and determined way.

Plan for the inevitable challenges that arise when you give learners choice and freedom to use it. Having a game plan for tackling avoidance or disruptive behaviors during the time students have an opportunity to move around the classroom is all part of the learning process for everyone. Be sure to include students in the brainstorming and troubleshooting process to get their invaluable input on any ideas, strategies, or solutions they may have that you might never have thought of.

Hold regular community meetings with your learners that spotlight movement and transitions in the classroom and how they are going. Chances are if moving around the classroom feels noisy and chaotic to you, it feels the same way to them and they want you to do something about it. Uncover why they might be waiting for you to handle things, rather than becoming inspired and empowered to act themselves. You could also let learners know that the freedom to make choices about their learning, to get up and move around the classroom, to gather supplies and collaborate on projects as they need to is not a right. Remind them that you reserve the right to revoke this privilege should their choices become problematic to the learning community.

Be consistent by explaining the purpose behind the messaging and holding students accountable to disruptive or time-wasting behaviors. When possible strategize with students what the accountability measures will look like. Clear and explicit demonstration of the expectations you and the learning community want to see, together with visual reminders and praise, generally work best.

Notice, name, and celebrate your community for making strides in the process. All of us appreciate specific feedback and encouragement to keep at something we are working on. You don't have to make it about how it pleases you, though. Simply noticing the effort and making it public can be praise enough.

Ultimately, it's important to let learners know that you trust them and that everybody is off task sometimes; it's normal and happens to adults all the time. The point is to recognize when this happens, note if and how it's affecting others, and find a way to focus and get back to work.

Since I have a lot of students and not a lot of space, how can I realistically make movement and transitions work under these restrictions?

Figuring out the answer to this question is part of practically every educator's greatest hits anthology.

First, reflect on what works and what improvements you'd like to see in the learning space you have currently designed. Then spend some time observing and jotting down a few notes about what movement and transitions look like during different parts of the day. Pay particular attention to when and where learners look and feel the most confined by the classroom layout. For example, see if you can pinpoint what seems to be causing the traffic jam every morning after the math lesson. Once you identify potential areas for growth, communicate your concerns to students, survey what they think, and learn more about their preferences for an ideal working space. Including their voices will also help to generate more imaginative solutions and develop the buy-in needed to make sure new layout ideas and routines are sustainable. When there are a lot of bodies in a small space, it will take ingenuity, empathy, commitment, and a few strategically designed changes to the classroom layout to make movement and transitions flow more effortlessly.

Here are a few tips from educators in your same predicament:

1. Create more space for movement by eliminating any clutter the best you can, especially in high traffic areas. Clutter often restricts movement and adds time and confusion to transitions that are supposed to be quick and seamless. The less clutter you have, the more space and time you can reclaim. The trick is for you and your learners to get into the habit of taking home or purging unnecessary items on a regular basis. Developing agreements and end-of-the-week routines to decrease clutter helps all learners practice this skill and start to build this important habit.

2. Try to maximize space in your layout for movement and transitions by decreasing the amount of furniture you have accumulated. For example, trading out a bulky book shelf for a slimmer model or six desks for a table just may offer you and your students a bit more room to operate. If moving around the classroom feels constrained and sometimes leads to disruptive behaviors, every inch matters.

3. Offer students more flexible seating options. Invite students to try out different spaces in the room to get work done, including sharing your personal table or desk space during student hours. When students have choices about where and how to get their work done, they become more engaged in their tasks and projects. They are less likely to waste time during the transition process because of their eagerness to begin their work.

4. Consider alternative writeable surfaces where students can potentially gather away from desks and tables to talk and share ideas. Position these surfaces strategically around the room in order to stretch out the classroom space and support movement goals. Access to writeable surfaces makes each classroom space more practical and user-friendly. Writeable surface options that don't take up desk space include small individual whiteboards, clipboards, Wizard Walls, a Post-it Super Sticky Dry Erase Surface, a Sherwin-Williams Sketch Pad Dry Erase Coating, and an Ideapad's paint and magnetic wall coverings. These innovative products will provide more options to move and work in just about any area of the classroom, giving your community a little more space to move and transition.

4

Considering the Social–Emotional Needs of Students in a Classroom Environment

Fourth-grade teacher Khalia got to school early to avoid Los Angeles traffic, but to also give her students the option to enter the classroom without delay. As with most mornings, Khalia readied the classroom by turning on lamps instead of the overhead lights, opening the window blinds, and playing light jazz or instrumental music on her smartphone. Once her fourth graders took care of a few morning upkeep routines—like watering plants, cleaning the whiteboard, dusting off technology, returning books to bins in the classroom library, or finishing up any homework assignments—they were free to settle into the classroom with a preferred activity. By inviting her students to start the day with a quiet preferred activity then transitioning to independent reading when the school bell rang, Khalia carved out a space to greet and make eye contact with a few students before the day's hustle and bustle. On this particular morning, she took a few minutes to settle in and prep her own teaching space. Once the bell rang, she greeted the rest of her class waiting just outside of the door, then made her way over to Tyreik. He had already removed his hat, stored his shoes, washed his hands, and was at his desk reading a graphic novel. His reader's notebook was nearby along with a few freshly

By taking a fresh look at how your space is an intellectual space in sync with implementing some physical tweaks, you can be more intentional in your practice, which is always a win for kids. Break the inertia now. Even taking the smallest step forward will begin a journey into the designer's mindset that can bolster the success of all students.

—REBECCA LOUISE HARE
AND ROBERT DILLON,
*THE SPACE: A GUIDE
FOR EDUCATORS*

sharpened pencils. Tyreik knew that his teacher would be by, so he waited his turn to briefly check in with her about his reading life. Khalia has always found this brief opportunity to connect with her students invaluable. It's during these moments that they show her another side to who they are. On this morning, Khalia pulled a chair close, smiled, and leaned in to say, "Tell me about the work you've been doing in your book, Tyreik." (See Figures 4.1–4.6.)

Figure 4.1 Fourth-grade classroom. Khalia used every available space, including her wall and cabinet door space, as tools for learning. She used decorative wooden letters above her storage cabinets to announce a sentiment that she hoped would ring true all year long and cultivate a sense of belonging. During the first trimester, she and her students got to know each other through writing and publishing narratives that revealed their hearts and minds. Displayed on her closet doors were charts, mentor examples, and student writing that spotlighted each stage of the writing process. Writers could visit this area at any time to utilize its resources and to support their own processes.

◀ ◀ ▲ Figures 4.2a, 4.2b, 4.2c, 4.2d Fourth-grade classroom. A sign posted just outside of the classroom read, "Shoeless learning." It invited all classroom visitors to go shoeless. A shoe cubby, step stools, and baskets were also provided to keep shoes organized for efficient arrivals and departures. There are lots of benefits to shoeless learning: students feel more comfortable, it helps to maintain a cleaner environment, it offers a quieter atmosphere, and it causes less wear and tear on classroom furniture and rugs. The origins of shoeless learning can be traced back to cold-weather Scandinavian countries where students shed their wet shoes before joining the classroom; in India where shoe removal in temples is symbolic of respect; in China where shoe removal keeps qi (pronounced *chee*) flowing through the body; and in England where going barefoot feels like being at home. The ten-plus years of research studies on shoeless learning show that students who remove their shoes at school are more calm, as well as participate and perform better academically (Heppell 2011).

Figures 4.3a and 4.3b Fourth-grade classroom. Khalia had the opportunity to create mood lighting by turning off the fluorescent lights and turning on lamps and accent lights. Her fourth graders said they felt calmer because it helped to create a less noisy and more peaceful place to think, read, and work together.

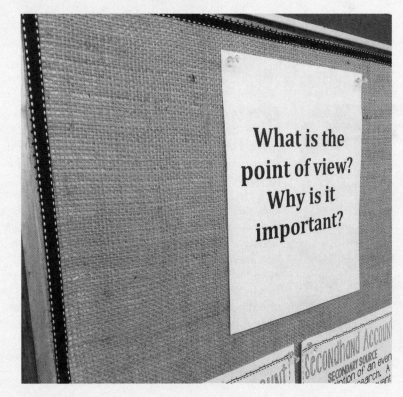

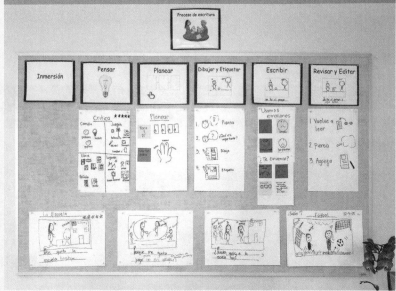

Figures 4.4a and 4.4b Primary and upper-grade classroom. For her classroom display boards, Khalia preferred neutral and earthy tones and textures to help keep the spotlight on student-created artifacts. Consider a borderless display board or use a simple reusable ribbon, which can hide seams while also adding sophistication.

Figures 4.5a and 4.5b Fourth-grade classroom. Khalia's pop-up lounge area had multiple, flexible seating options that could be used in a variety of configurations. The furniture could also be moved around to create a totally new space in another area of the room. Check out the photo image she posted for students of how the space should look after cleanup time. Cleanup monitors could check the image and quickly restore the space based on the photo support.

Figures 4.6a and 4.6b Sixth-grade ELA middle school classroom. Aimee removed the legs from a table to alter the height. She then added pillows so learners could kneel or sit on the floor while working. The pillow covers were removable for easy cleaning. Aimee offered a few height-adjustable standing desks as a sit/stand option for her students. She spent the better part of a semester inviting each learner to rotate through the different seating choices and work spaces to build a sense of their learning preferences.

Connecting Social-Emotional Needs with Design Elements

By now you might be thinking to yourself, will rearranging my room to provide more flexible seating options really decrease stress, increase student engagement, and bolster test scores? The answer is yes! Take a moment to consider where you feel the most productive and why that is. What conditions need to be in place for you to keep focused, feel creative, and be energized? What will make you, yes *you*, excited and eager to arrive to your work space each day and teach your heart out?

Most of us personalize our work space, no matter how small, with a few touchstone items like photos, cards, plants, and tokens of appreciation that tell a narrative about who we are or who we are striving to become. We lean on those items for comfort, encouragement, and inspiration. What about our students? What might be comforting, encouraging, and inspiring to them? What conditions might make their learning environment socially, emotionally, and physically responsive to their learning needs? Let's take a closer look at some of the images from Khalia's classroom. Khalia paid attention to details like these:

- *Comfort.* On the day I visited, Khalia's classroom had soft music playing in the background. Right away, I noticed some students shuffled around in socks while others were spread out on the floor or working in small groups across the room. Some students worked independently along the perimeters of the room, with partners in chairs, or on a couch. A few others worked near a standing desk while Khalia led a reading lesson with students at a table in the far corner of the room. Although the room was buzzing, the sounds felt productive, measured, and organized. A short time later, one of her students invited me to take my shoes off. I did and ended up staying awhile.

- *Cleanliness.* Khalia took pictures of the most commonly used spaces in her room, printed them out, and posted them in their corresponding areas so that her students were aware of and started to feel more comfortable about the expectation of what the space should look like at the end of the day. "Having those photos changed everything about our cleanup routines for my students. The photos served as a guide for putting things back together quickly. By the middle of the year, my students didn't need them anymore, so we just stored them away to show any new students who arrived," Khalia said.

- *Color.* Khalia's room had a hip, coffee shop–like atmosphere. Over the summer, she and her mentor extraordinaire, Rosanne López (whose classroom images in kindergarten are also featured in this book), made some decisions about color. She chose to use a variety of browns and grays as base colors for her wall, sink, and furniture. She also used green, blue, and terracotta hues as accent colors, which are represented in plants, pillows, containers, lamp shades, and rugs. She was relieved when her students responded positively to the colors and to the space. They continue to tinker with it, moving tables and rugs around to make the space feel like a home base for everyone.

∘ *__Lighting.__* In order to decrease stress and anxiety, Khalia also created a comfy, safe space for students to visit and work in when they needed a quiet moment. It included a mini couch, an end table, a few plants, and some accent lighting. Being in this little nook felt calming, especially when the overhead lights were dimmed. "It just feels better in the classroom when the main lights are off, and I open up the blinds. If my students need more light, I also have lamps around the room," Khalia said.

Khalia does not have a background in interior design, but the decisions she made about her classroom environment were informed by basic design principles and the desire for balance and harmony in her physical spaces. More importantly, she used what she knew about learning and her learners: when students are in an environment where they feel respected and emotionally supported, they are more engaged. "To learn, children and adolescents need to feel safe and supported. Without these conditions, the mind reverts to a focus on survival. Educators in high-performing, high-poverty schools have long recognized the critical importance of providing a healthy, safe, and supportive classroom and school environment" (Parrett and Budge 2012, 110). A bill of rights for students must include "food if hungry, clean clothes if needed, medical attention when necessary, counseling and other family services as required, and most of all caring adults who create an atmosphere of sincere support for the students' well-being *and* academic success" (Parrett and Budge 2012, 110). When educators use design as a tool to create a supportive atmosphere for learning, they are in effect taking up a call to action. Implementing a few basic design features—like light, color, sound, and natural elements—supports children's thinking and learning experiences as well as creates a more aesthetically pleasing space to make mistakes and to grow.

Light

Light is a design element that makes things visible. Designers often use lighting to create mood, to call attention to the shape of objects, and to accommodate the variety of activities that take place in a single space. Educators also use light to illuminate the overall classroom space and to keep students alert.

There are three main types of indoor lighting that educators can consider when creating a space that feels warm and conducive to learning. Ambient lighting illuminates the entire classroom space for safety and visibility. Task lighting generally illuminates smaller areas of the classroom that may be harder to reach with ambient lighting. Accent lighting illuminates and spotlights particular items or projects that you want to draw attention to. Lighting needs can vary depending on task or project, so designers and many teachers find that layering all three types of lighting allows for more comfort and flexibility in the classroom. (See Figures 4.7–4.10.)

Whether you have big, bright windows that let in lots of natural light or a classroom with plenty of artificial lighting, according to the Heschong Mahone study, well-lit spaces can significantly influence reading, math, vocabulary, and science test scores (Barrett et al. 2015). During some parts of the day, educators even turn off their ambient, overhead lights and work only by natural and accent lighting if possible. They claim that students are often calmer and do some of

Figures 4.7a and 4.7b First-grade classroom. Shayla's classroom featured lamps all around the room, but most students enjoyed reading in the well-lit, cozy classroom library space under sunlit windows.

Figure 4.8 Third-grade classroom. Jamaica's classroom had one window facing a playground and another facing green space. Student preferences for seating varied day to day and by activity. On this morning, Albert and Leonard made a choice to write together at a coffee table not too far away from all the morning sunlight streaming in.

their best thinking when the main overhead lighting is decreased or turned off entirely. Research backs up this claim. Studies suggest that limiting the amount of light or turning the lights off and only using natural or full-spectrum lightbulbs supports more rational decision-making and allows for better negotiations (Xu and Labroo 2014).

Figure 4.9 Third-grade classroom. Using a small desk lamp allowed light to be cast on a specific area. Task lighting options can be controlled by students. They also create greater contrast for the words written on the page, which makes reading easier on the eyes.

Figure 4.10 Sixth-grade middle school classroom. Aimee's classroom building design was well lit. It included large windows that opened up to green space, built-in windows, framed doorway entrances, and retractable ceiling skylights. Often needing to incorporate technology into her lessons, she had to balance when to use natural light and when to use artificial light.

Color

Color is an integral design element that appeals to our sense of sight. Color activates our mood, feelings, and perceptions of the world around us in different ways. Designers use color to evoke emotion, create associations, and get a reaction or response. They use color to help define the purpose of a space and whether it's meant to be used for relaxation, entertainment, collaboration, or study. Educators use color to create beautiful, inviting, and dynamic learning environments that foster productivity, communication, and collaboration (see Figures 4.11–4.14). It's important to acknowledge that "not everyone thinks about or experiences color in the same way. The meaning and symbolism we associate with different colors are influenced a great deal by the cultural and societal groups we identify with" (Kliever 2016). Take the color blue for example. In Middle Eastern culture blue signifies safety and protection. In many religions blue is the sign of hope and good health. In Western culture, blue signifies feelings of melancholy, and we often refer to feeling blue or having the blues when we are depressed or in low spirits (Kliever 2016).

There is a lot of anecdotal research on color and countless debates about how colors are perceived by the brain and what their impact is on mood, clarity of thought, and energy level (Englebrecht 2003). It could be helpful for all educators to learn a little about color theory, the psychology of color, and how colors work together to affect mood and create aesthetically pleasing classroom spaces.

Color has three characteristics: hue, value, and intensity. *Hue* refers to the dominant color family—yellow, orange, red, violet, blue, and green are considered hues. It also refers to mixtures like blue-green. *Value* refers to the lightness or darkness of a hue. *Intensity*, also known as saturation, refers to the purity of a color on a range from pure to gray. When they decide on colors for a design project, interior designers typically recommend choosing a color palette that combines three hues—one dominant and two accent colors that typically work to balance out the dominant color. Also, rather than displaying each color equally, designers use a common practice known as the 60-30-10 rule, which dictates that your dominant hue accounts for 60 percent of the color in the design space while the other two accent colors make up the remaining 30 percent and 10 percent. An alternative interior design rule uses one dominant hue and a variety of shades (darker) and tints (lighter) of the chosen hue so that you avoid a rainbow color scheme that doesn't feel connected. "The key to creating ready-to-learn environments, is a variety of colors and a range of color intensity, including some hues used as way-finders and culture-builders in common areas" (Fielding 2006).

Figure 4.15 shows a list of ten colors commonly used in design and our typical associations with each (Lischer 2018). "Researchers have suggested that color associations may have been formulated early in human history when man associated dark blue with night, and therefore, passivity and bright yellow with sunlight and arousal" (Grossman and Wisenblit 1999, 80).

Figure 4.11 Kindergarten classroom. "I prefer to use muted tones and earthy hues throughout the classroom. I use baskets and wooden crates for storage along with other natural materials and fabric to support my color scheme. Our display boards are simply designed with textured borders in neutral shades to highlight the color choices made by students," Rosanne said.

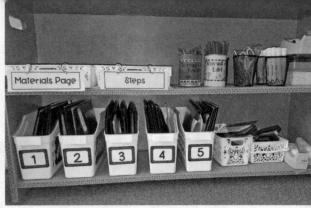

Figure 4.14 First-grade classroom. You don't need to completely overhaul a space to make a dramatic impact. Lots of teachers take a DIY route to keep costs down by adding a fresh coat of paint to existing furniture. Shayla took her stand-alone bookcase home over the summer, sanded a few edges, and painted it to complement her color scheme.

Figure 4.12 First-grade classroom. "Cool colors with splashes of warm colors and soft lighting make the space feel interesting and comfortable for my students. It makes me feel good too. I also like to use music, essential oil diffusers, plants, and fabrics to make the classroom feel like home, so they can relax and learn," Shayla said.

Figures 4.13a and 4.13b Middle school classroom. Aimee had neutral tones on the walls and carpeting, then she used different shades of blue to add color that was visually appealing. She also distinguished her different English language arts periods by color-coding the file boxes that held student portfolios. "Before designing my space, I did some independent research on colors that are calming and stabilizing for preteens and adolescents. I learned that preteens and adolescents' brains respond to muted colors and calming tones like light blues or greens. The shift in my thinking about classroom design has really made a positive impact on student engagement," she said.

Figure 4.15 Colors, Associations, and Classroom Recommendations

Color	Positive Associations	Classroom Recommendations
Red	Energy, power, and passion	Reds can be used to warm up spaces and make them feel more intimate.
Orange	Excitement, friendliness, and innovation	Oranges are commonly used as an accent color to draw attention. They can be stimulating and evoke enthusiasm.
Yellow	Happiness, optimism, and creativity	Yellows can be used in combination with another neutral hue in rooms with lots of natural light to create a calm and peaceful environment.
Green	Growth, health, hope	Greens can be used to soothe and relax us; think of celebrity "green rooms." Greens are also easiest on our sight because we don't have to adjust our eyes when it hits our retina.
Blue	Serenity, security, and trust	Blues can be used to evoke calm and clarity. Studies have shown it supports productivity.
Purple	Imagination, sophistication, and wisdom	Purples can be used as an accent color in combination with other hues to add complexity and sophistication.
Gray	Neutrality, intelligence, and strength	Grays can be used to add calm to spaces.
Brown	Warmth, earthiness, and reliability	Browns are typically thought of as a utilitarian color and can be used to evoke authenticity and naturalness in the classroom.
Black	Power, elegance, and authority	Black can be used to highlight projects or items that you want to draw attention to.
White	Simplicity, cleanliness, and purity	White is great for helping to define a space, but too much can be perceived as dull and sterile.

When you think about modifying the color scheme in your classroom, consider some of these color associations and recommendations to help you make simple adjustments. You can start by identifying the dominant color palette in your space. If you'd like help determining the existing color scheme in your classroom, simply visit the Canva website at https://www.canva.com and upload a picture of your classroom. They will use the hues in your photograph to generate a customized color palette. Once you know your starting point, you have some options about where to go next when it comes to color changes in your classroom. Another idea is to think about requesting a new paint job over the summer or start incrementally on your own. Use your knowledge of color theory to remove items that don't match your color scheme and to add items like rugs, storage, and pillows that fit within your color plan or the color palette you have chosen to use.

Sound

Children are affected by noise and poor classroom acoustics in different ways. Excessive noise can be a particular problem for students that have learning challenges and hearing loss. Research out of the University of Salford, England, found that unwanted noises from sources such as students on the playground or in the hallway, heating or air conditioning units, and audiovisual equipment negatively affected the way students learn (Barrett et al. 2015). According to the National Research Council's Committee to Review and Assess the Health and Productivity Benefits of Green Schools, "Good acoustical quality in classrooms is critical for student learning. Research has shown that noise exposure affects educational outcomes and provides evidence of mechanisms that explain the effects of noise on learning" (2007, 92).

One way educators might begin to create a quiet and calming learning space might be to pay particular attention to distracting noises that surround the classroom and find ways to decrease them. Consider solutions like these:

- adding rugs to tiled floors

- keeping windows and doors closed

- identifying the noisy and quiet parts of the classroom

- using noise-cancelling headphones

- setting up small or individual table spaces away from groups, near the corners of the room

- using nontraditional learning spaces like hallway alcoves, school gardens, and kitchens. (Ask teaching assistants or parent volunteers to help with supervision in these areas.)

See Figures 4.16–4.18.

Figures 4.16a and 4.16b Kindergarten classroom. As a way to cut down on background noise (any sound that makes it hard to hear) and reverberation (echo), Rosanne and her teaching partner, Christine, both invited their students to store shoes in cubbies near the entryway prior to entering the classroom. Students wore socks from home or were provided with socks. "Going shoeless and having alternative, flexible seating options make a difference with noise levels in our classroom," Rosanne said.

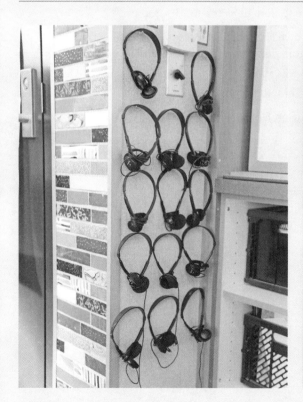

◀◀ **Figure 4.17** Middle school classroom. In her English language arts classes, Aimee employed a checkout system for students to use regular and noise-canceling headphones to modify noise levels in the classroom that affected their thinking and well-being.

◀ **Figure 4.18** Second-grade classroom. Using noise-canceling headphones and playing soft background music on portable devices can decrease the volume of a busy classroom for learners who prefer a quieter work environment.

Natural Elements

Designers use natural items or biophilic elements of nature (fresh flowers and plants) to help us feel more connected to the outdoors. Educators use natural elements and textures to spark interest and creativity in the classroom. Research finds that exposure to nature or natural elements "promotes attention restoration, memory, competence, supportive social groups, self-discipline, moderates stress, improves behaviors and symptoms of ADHD and was even associated with higher standardized test scores" (McCormick 2017, 4).

What are some ways to incorporate more nature or natural elements into your classroom?

- Open up any windows that might look out onto green space.

- Set up a nature table, art table, or dedicate a shelf space to store and marvel at nature items. Encourage students to bring in things to contribute, touch, and interact with more closely (e.g., sticks, pinecones, leaves, bark, seeds, and shells). In my own primary classroom, we often composed still-life arrangements with items from nature. Students spent time honing their observation skills while pencil drawing and shading three-dimensional objects.

- Invite parents to take turns donating flowers, plants, or even succulents that can be broken off and replanted into jars and placed near windows. Local gardens and nurseries have also been known to donate plants to classrooms.

- Consider repurposing materials you already own like metal tins, glass jars, and baskets that use natural fibers as a way to store items and reduce the amount of plastic in the classroom.

- Bring in small water features like fountains to create soothing sounds.

- Use tree stumps as flexible seating options. (See Figures 4.19–4.21.)

Figure 4.19 Fifth-grade classroom. Jamaica decided on a green and gray color scheme for her fifth-grade library space, largely due to the oversized green comfy chair that a friend donated to her classroom. She complemented the color scheme with a few indoor plants and light-colored furniture, which helped to keep the space light and airy.

Figure 4.20 Kindergarten classroom. Rosanne used color, pattern (a visual print), and texture (how something feels) on walls, ceilings, floors, and furnishings to create uncommonly beautiful spaces that appealed to the senses. She also used color-filled textiles from the parts of the world her students were from to promote and honor cultural stories and traditions.

Figures 4.21a, 4.21b, 4.21c First-grade classroom. Shayla created interest and brought novelty to her classroom space by adding natural elements around the room on shelves, near supplies, and even in lieu of a boring rubber door stopper.

Teaching into Design Elements

Reimagining your classroom design can feel overwhelming and is often easier to do over the summer, winter, or spring break when your brain has more creative space to dedicate to these ideas. Anything feels possible and more manageable once the brain has had the opportunity to rejuvenate and rest. Start with a goal and a few small steps to meet it. Rearrange furniture so that your students can better see each another, add a plant, or add a desk lamp. Once your students arrive and see what you have done, it will encourage you to do more. You'll also start to notice that some of the changes you are making are positively impacting the learning needs of your students. As you strive to use your classroom design in strategic ways to support learning goals, some of the questions you'll want to start thinking about answering include

- How can I use design elements to support the social and emotional well-being of my students?

- How will these design elements motivate my students to take more ownership of their learning?

- How will incorporating these design elements support my students with attention challenges?

Although using the elements of design to make classroom environment decisions won't solve every teaching and learning challenge you come across, it can be a tangible starting point for addressing the diverse needs of your learners with patience, empathy, and compassion.

Here's an example of a lesson I might teach about choosing a productive work space, using the architecture of minilessons defined by the Teachers College Reading and Writing Project (Calkins 2003).

A SAMPLE LESSON: CHOOSING A PRODUCTIVE WORK SPACE

Connection (2–4 minutes)

We've been talking a lot lately about getting to know ourselves as learners and what we need to do our best thinking and learning. We all learn in different ways so what feels right to you may be distracting to someone else and vice versa. I have been watching many of you lately make some hard decisions about where to sit and get your work done. It's not always easy to make those decisions, and at times it can feel overwhelming. There are lots of factors to consider. So, today I'd like to offer you a strategy that I use when I need to be productive.

Teach (3–5 minutes)

When I have to meet a deadline and want to be productive at school or at home, there are three things I like to have control over to help me think and work more efficiently. Here are my "Top 3." (I produce a sticky note with my ideas and unveil them one at a time.)

1. **Quiet.** I don't need it to be totally quiet, but I do need to be able to think and work, so I try to find a space away from people who are talking to get my work done.

2. **Light.** Since I can't see in the dark, I have to be in a space where I can clearly see my work. I don't need it to be super bright, just bright enough so I am not squinting or holding the paper up to my face. At home I sit near a lamp while I am working.

3. **Comfort.** I prefer to work in a comfy chair or on a sofa. If I am at home, I like to have a cup of hot coffee or tea near me.

So that's my Top 3. When I find a space to work, I usually have to make some adjustments so that it is kinda quiet, well lit, and comfy. If I can't figure out how to be productive in the work space I choose, then I'll most likely have to look for another work space. However, when my Top 3 are in place, my brain knows it is time to get some work done, and I can relax and begin my process. (See Figure 4.22.)

Figure 4.22 Teacher Top 3

Engagement (2–4 minutes)

You probably noticed by now that there are some things that help you do your best thinking and learning during independent work time. Take a minute to think about what those things are. Then I will ask you to make a quick sketch on a sticky note and share your Top 3 with someone sitting next to you.

(Listen in on students as they share with one another and try to capture any responses that might be helpful to consider as your room environment evolves.) *Let's come back together to share out a few more ideas. (Jot down a list of student responses to help others get more ideas; see Figures 4.23a–4.23c).*

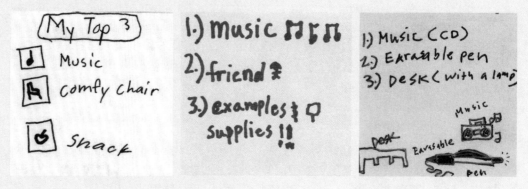

Figures 4.23a, 4.23b, 4.23c Student Samples of Top 3

Top 3 Responses from Class

- Music

- A comfy chair

- Floor seating

Closing (1–2 minutes)

I'd like you to carry the sticky note you created with your own Top 3 work space preferences around with you for the rest of the week so that you can self-check that you are making choices that fit with what you know about yourself as a learner. You can leave it on the cover or put it on the inside cover of a notebook or folder that you are using. Sometimes it is also helpful to have a partner hold you accountable to your decisions and ask you how it's going. So, after you leave the meeting area and set up for math, quickly share the Top 3 things you need to have in place to do your best thinking with your partner. Be sure you leave some time each day this week to check in and discuss how the work spaces you have been selecting are working or not working out for you.

A QUICK GUIDE TO DESIGN ELEMENTS

Design Element

LIGHT

Questions to Consider

How do I define *proper* lighting in my classroom?

How could varying the levels of lighting support

- alertness

- focus

- mood

- confidence

- productivity

What are the issues with fluorescent lighting?

What other type of lighting is there besides fluorescent lighting?

What are some ways I can adjust brightness?

Potential Challenges

Lack of windows in the classroom

Nonopening blinds in the room

Health concerns:

- eye strain

- glare

- headaches

Sensitivity to the buzzing of fluorescent lights

What This Might Look/Sound Like

Use light fixtures like floor or desk lamps in areas of the classroom that need more light.

Use a mix of natural lighting and lamps to create calmness and support mood regulation.

Open window blinds to let in more natural light.

Use lamp shades or a flame-retardant cloth to filter harsh light on ceiling.

Dim or turn off fluorescent lights when reentering the classroom after a specialty class or recess.

Design Element
COLOR

Questions to Consider

How do I define a color-rich environment?

What role does color play in student learning?

What impact does color have on emotion?

How do I use color to stimulate participation?

How do I use color to support information retention?

Which colors seem to benefit student learning most?

How can I use hues as "way-finders" and "culture builders" in the classroom? (Fielding 2006)

Potential Challenges

Overstimulation or large amounts of bright colors

Furnishings (desks, chairs, bookcases) usually selected based on functionality and cost

Mismatched colors or hodgepodge of colors on walls, flooring, and furniture

What This Might Look/Sound Like

Choose a color scheme that matches your purpose (typically two or three hues) and stick with it.

Discard, sell on Craigslist, or donate items that do not match your color plan and purpose for the space.

Consider keeping walls a neutral color and adding splashes of color with furnishing choices.

Assign tasks to certain colors. For example, blue chairs and pillows are for reading and relaxing near the classroom library. Orange chairs and stools are for collaborating with friends/peers on a project or assignment.

Design Element
SOUND

Questions to Consider

How do I define quiet in my classroom?

How can I support learners that need quiet?

How can I create quiet work spaces?

How can I make space for quieter work periods across the day?

Potential Challenges

Noises cause students to feel

- unfocused

- distracted

- overwhelmed

- frustrated

Students have difficulty hearing the teacher or peers, even when sitting in a small group

You can't open windows due to loud outdoor noises

Fan that regulates classroom temperature is noisy

What This Might Look/Sound Like

Create individual work spaces throughout the room.

Play soft background music.

Create space on the agenda for reflection activities and mindfulness techniques.

Reduce visual noise:

- clutter

- print on walls

- digital (screens)

Design Element

NATURAL ELEMENTS

Some Possible Visual Resources

Questions to Consider

How am I defining natural elements?

What natural elements might work best for students at my grade level?

Will my students take care of these elements?

Potential Challenges

Nature items can trigger allergies

Plant upkeep can be costly

Nature items can be distracting

What This Might Look/Sound Like

Consider a small budget for indoor plants, to foster creativity and productivity.

Open up your window treatments. Direct views of nature and sunlight have positive benefits on learning (Ulrich 1984).

Use images of nature and artificial plants, especially when plants (allergies) and window views (unsafe or nonexistent) are not feasible.

Consider natural airflow, regulating room temperature to improve comfort and energy in the classroom.

Incorporate natural sounds (ocean waves) and smells (essential oils) into the classroom. These help to contribute to a multisensory learning experience that the brain likes when it learns new things.

Take a Break

Visit the nature Table.

Take a short walk outside.

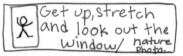

Get up, stretch and look out the window / nature photo.

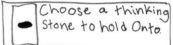

Choose a thinking stone to hold onto.

Care and Maintenance: Keeping track of each of the work spaces and items that seem to attract the most dust and germs is a must. Use durable and removable covers for furnishings like seats, pillows, couches, and cushions, and ask your families if they would also be willing to sign up and take turns washing the class linens across the school year.

Be sure to assign housekeeping tasks to student monitors and allow them to teach the job to peers as the year progresses. Teach a watering monitor how to care for both indoor and outdoor plants by designing a watering schedule. Light monitors can be tasked with energy conservation responsibilities at the start and end of each day. Noise monitors should make sure windows and doors are latched closed, headphones are returned to storage containers, and the shoe cubby area is kept organized and swept clean of dirt, sand, or those pesky wood chips each day.

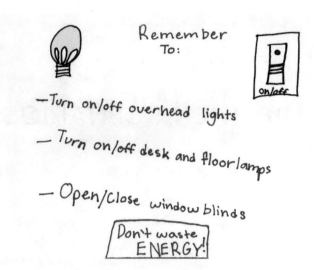

Remember To:
—Turn on/off overhead lights
— Turn on/off desk and floor lamps
— Open/Close window blinds
Don't waste ENERGY!

If your school is purchasing new rugs or furniture, woohoo! Volunteer to be included in the school's council meetings about on-site, decision-making processes, especially when it affects the color and variety of products being purchased. Also, consider requesting rugs in solid colors so that you have more control over the color scheme, and choose tightly woven area rugs instead of plush carpets that trap dirt more easily and are harder to keep clean.

IF–THEN SCENARIOS

If I want to consider design elements, where should I start?

Before you even think about the light, color, sound, or natural elements in your class-room, do yourself a *huge* favor and begin by decluttering your space. Donate, eliminate, or remove items that are bulky, take up lots of space, or you and your students don't use often enough. This may mean enlisting support from your custodial team and getting rid of a table or two. Also, consider losing the file cabinet filled with papers you haven't looked at in years. Once all of the clutter that is piled up in plain view or hidden away in closets is cleared away, the easiest and most impactful starting point is to see what you can do to vary light and sound levels.

It seems like this could be a costly endeavor to think about design elements. I want to follow the research, but don't have a design or furniture budget. I will have to pay for the things I want out of my own pocket. What can I do?

I understand your predicament and encourage you to start with the elements that you can make adjustments to without digging into your savings account. All of this work is more about changing your mindset about your space versus fancy furniture. It doesn't cost anything to open up the blinds and let in the natural light for most or part of the day. Make plans to alter room lighting (turn off the fluorescent lighting) by opening up windows if you have them and by adding more light to darker spaces in the room.

 Make sure you regularly check your school and district storage depots or basement for unused furniture. Ask your principal if you can swap out chairs so the colors, sizes, or shapes match. Ask parents or the PTA for household donations. They might have just what you are looking for. Snap a photo of what you are after and create a wish list to share with others. On your wish list, include things like lamps, bulbs, and washable pillow coverings. Remember, it doesn't have to be all-or-nothing. What's important is that you engage in conversations with your students and families about what you are trying to do and why you are doing it. They will no doubt be thrilled to see your eagerness (and relentlessness) and want to figure out ways to support the extraordinary learning opportunities taking place in your classroom.

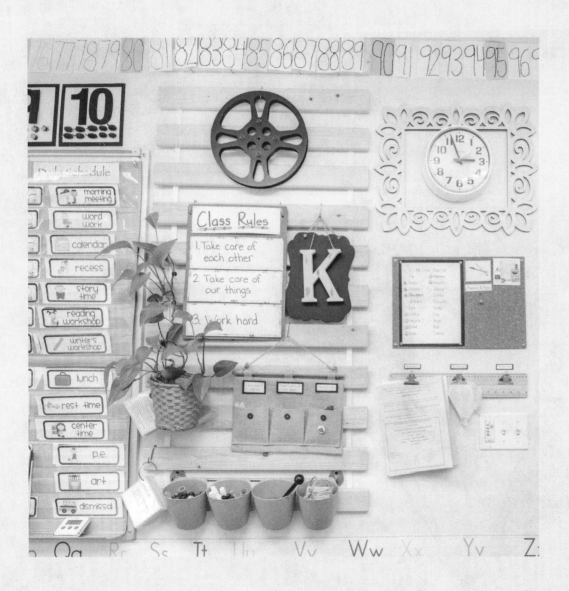

5

One Teacher's Journey with Strategic Classroom Design

What must it feel like for a veteran teacher to transfer to a new school, teach a different grade from last year, and have to set up shop in a temporary, portable third-grade classroom without furniture—just two weeks before school begins? Jamaica came to some realizations very quickly:

- She didn't really need a lot of furniture.
- She didn't really need a teacher's desk.
- She needed a strategic plan.

First, she met with her new principal, Sarah, and got approval to reimagine a learning environment using research-based design elements and lots of flexible seating opportunities. Then she made friends with the summer custodial team. She needed their support, too. They had important knowledge about the site, tools, and a sturdy hand truck to assist in moving furniture around the classroom. Next, she gave me a call; we spoke about goals, a few fears, what she wanted most for her learners, and what she wanted to get better at in her own practice. Shortly after, we met in the space, walked every inch, dreamed a bit, then came back to reality. By sketching a plan, we brainstormed how to do more with less. We asked ourselves, "How might we create a space that felt calm, welcoming, organized, engaging, and collaborative to everyone—all while on a budget?"

> *An environment is a living, changing system. More than the physical space, it includes the way time is structured and the roles we are expected to play. It conditions how we feel, think, and behave; and it dramatically affects the quality of our lives.*
>
> —JIM GREENMAN,
> *CARING SPACES,
> LEARNING PLACES*

Calm

Jamaica's entire classroom was painted off-white, which blurred the floor-to-ceiling lines and gave the illusion of being more spacious. She chose to keep the room feeling light, airy, and calm by opening up blinds, turning off the lights, and using earthy tones as her color scheme. She brought in a few beige area rugs from her former classroom and purchased a few blue and brown pillow covers for students to use in the meeting and library areas. "The students enjoyed having pillows so much they typically ended up using them to cushion a chair, lean against, and occasionally just to hold and have something to embrace while reading in the classroom library or listening to a read-aloud," Jamaica said. By altering light, decreasing background noises, and adding elements of nature and comfort, Jamaica created a space that was appealing to each of the senses.

Welcoming

A gathering space for community meetings was a priority for Jamaica. She wanted the space to feel welcoming, to accommodate everyone comfortably, and to feel intimate enough to make eye contact or use lowered voices. She also wanted the space to be able to handle hard conversations that might arise across the school year. This was their classroom. "This space belonged to all of us. It's where we met, worked, and laughed together all year long. Students, even former ones, are always welcome to come back for a visit and tell stories of their far-away adventures."

Organized

"We used lots of bins, baskets, containers, and labels to help stay organized," Jamaica said. This year, Jamaica tried placing a few small, transparent, and shoe-sized storage bins near her teaching and planning work areas to help sort all of the school memos, bulletins, and paperwork. Keeping clutter to a minimum became a priority, and many students found a talent for it, always making sure things were returned to their right places and that miscellaneous items were placed in Jamaica's box near her computer.

Jamaica's students learned the art of periodically sorting their own supplies and work into baskets, folders, and containers. Each student had a personal cubby that held books, reading logs, and English language arts and math materials.

Engaging

By learning how to hand over more responsibility to her students, Jamaica cultivated higher levels of student engagement across the day and school year. "As the year progressed, my students learned to relax into the routines of learning, making better choices, anticipating the challenges of where to sit and whom to sit next to, which supplies they needed, and where or whom to go to if they needed support. We also made a lot of progress with our decision-making in a short period of time. Some students realized, for example, that the area with our coffee table and two comfy chairs felt a bit too distracting for them. They made the decision to work in an individual space with a clipboard so that they could concentrate better." By making better seating choices, many of Jamaica's students worked on tasks for longer periods of time and began to feel more accomplished in their efforts. "I believe they were less distracted by ambient noise and peers because they had found a comfortable, just-right space to settle into, and they became more engaged in their work. I think it helped, too, that all of us learned to become a little more aware of each other while sharing the work space. We tried to be quieter for each other sometimes and it worked out."

Collaborative

Jamaica made it a priority to provide opportunities for students to get to know her and one another. It was important to her that each learner felt seen and heard. Getting to know each other early in the school year is an essential part of growing and sustaining collaborative structures. The more we learn about how our friends like to communicate and function, the more comfortable it becomes to work in diverse groupings and to have positive and productive learning experiences. Jamaica used part of daily whole-group meetings to connect as a community of learners. During these meetings, students were invited to share their stories, contribute ideas, help design and discuss classroom agreements, and troubleshoot rituals and routines together. Throughout the day, students also had opportunities to build relationships with one another by participating in small-group tasks and working with different groups of peers on projects. To collaborate effectively, creating buy-in is essential. "We have got to be all-in for one another," Jamaica said. "I teach strategies for sharing ideas in respectful and kind ways. We practice waiting our turn and active listening . . . The work feels slow at times, but it is well worth it. When there are opportunities to explore and work together, the classroom seems to be more alive and learning seems to be more fun."

Spaces

Whole-Group Meeting Area

Jamaica wanted a meeting space flexible enough to hold a variety of learning experiences. This space served as a main teaching area, community meeting space, project space, and small-group work space.

AFTER WITH LEARNERS

AFTER

BEFORE

Small-Group Work Spaces

Once she dedicated space for a classroom library, Jamaica imagined using the perimeters of the room for small-group spaces. "The comfy chair and coffee table lounge spot quickly became a favorite space for students."

AFTER

AFTER WITH LEARNERS

Individual Work Spaces

Jamaica was fascinated to discover how quickly the students made the space their own. "At first the students would find a spot and start working. Once I introduced a few comfort items like pillows and lap trays, they took full advantage. No fights erupted but it was intense for a while."

AFTER WITH LEARNERS

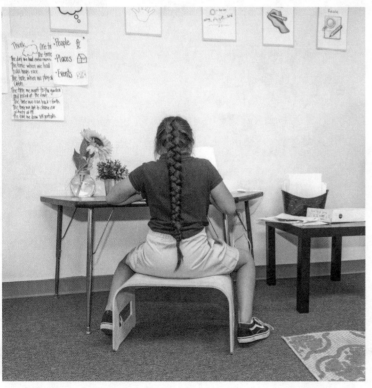

Teacher Space

"In the past, my desk usually served as a place to hold electronic devices or to collect piles of paperwork! When I do sit and plan in the mornings or after school, I usually spread out all of my materials across a table.

"Since all of the surface spaces now belong to my students, it has been a big adjustment for me to organize and put away all of my materials when I finish planning so that they have access to the space if they want to use it.

"Using cabinets, baskets, and bins to manage all of my work materials has been challenging but completely doable when I set aside a little time and attention each day.

"My work space now looks like their work space. I was very good at staying organized early in the year. I cleaned up the space at the end of each day, putting my materials in bins and back in my cubby (storage cabinet).

"As the year has progressed, I have accumulated more 'stuff' and it has been more challenging to keep my things organized.

"However, if the kids want to use a space that has my paperwork on it, they know that they can simply make a pile with any books or papers and push it to the center of the table.

"Even when I am at the table with them, they can sit in any seat, even my office chair! I love saying that, because it highlights that my kids have control over the space . . . every space is ours this year, not mine and theirs.

"Just as I expect and give my students time to get organized and to manage materials, I also need to remember to do the same for myself."

Makerspace

"I was hesitant and unsure about creating a makerspace. I kept it simple by gathering up all of my tape, scissors, drawing materials, paper clips, and popsicle sticks. When I saw the assortment of repurposed materials at the 'Two Bit Circus' organization and supply center, I thought of our science unit on force and motion. I knew my students would be able to use items like tubes, boards for ramps, and weighted balls, marbles, and small cars."

Classroom Library

Jamaica decided to build a library space underneath the picture window.

"I included different seating options but left a wide-open space since students seem to enjoy reading while lying on the floor." She used Ikea cabinets with wide compartments and see-through shelving to give the illusion of more space.

AFTER WITH LEARNERS

BEFORE

Content-Area Exploration

Jamaica created a central storage area along the back of the room by pushing three metal shelving units together to house materials students could access—math collections, tools, and games.

Jamaica used wooden baskets from the local donations store for storing items. They looked nice, were sturdy, and were easy for students to transport to other areas of the classroom if they needed more space.

AFTER

AFTER WITH LEARNERS

Multimedia Learning Spaces

The charging cart made it easy for students to find their assigned and fully charged laptops, tablets, and earbuds. Once they had all of the supplies they needed, each learner found a space in the room to work with a small group or alone.

Art Atelier

Jamaica's art atelier was housed on a mobile storage unit, so it could be rolled into any area, even outdoors in the school garden during an arts rotation. Most of the time, though, it was located near the center of the classroom so that her artists could find mixed-media materials to use on projects and/or assignments.

"It's been lovely to have the art supplies out in the room. They are beautiful to look at and I've also noticed that my students are more likely to use the colored pencils, oil pastels, and watercolors to enhance their science notebook work and social studies projects because those supplies are now visible and accessible."

Movement

Accessing Supplies

In the past, Jamaica tried both individual pencil boxes and table supply boxes to help learners keep track of supplies. This year with her new layout in place it made more sense to design a centralized supply system that housed most of the common items students would need—paper, pens, pencils, scissors, tape, clips, and so on.

"If they really have to keep a particular pen or pencil, they just keep it in their cubby; otherwise all supplies make it back to the central supply area when it is time to tidy up," says Jamaica.

Students could stand up and move to get what they needed at any time across the day.

Transitions

"I had to consider how it felt to enter the room. I wanted it to feel open. Also, I had to be certain that all of the routes for movement and travel were accessible to my student in a wheelchair. By creating strategic learning areas, and having mobile storage, like bookshelves on wheels, the paths for movement are clear and wide. My students have multiple ways to access any area of the room, and in some cases, they can easily move furniture out of the way to create more space.

"Before each transition, I give learners explicit directions or scaffolding. When they leave the meeting area, I dismiss students in small groups. I provide additional time for children who have a more difficult time making the transition. For those students, I provide quick oral and/or visual reminders."

Design

Light

Jamaica's windows let in tons of natural light, so she turned off the artificial lights whenever possible. She preferred using table and floor lamps and the natural light from the windows whenever possible.

"I have two small lamps low to the ground and a Himalayan rock salt lamp on the stand-up table. I keep the lights dim most of the day. Typically, I turn them on only in the afternoon to boost energy. There are twinkling lights around the colored pencils on the center bookcase that are decorative. There are lamps near almost every table and side table in the room."

Jamaica had an additional perk just outside one of her windows. Corn, watermelons, squash, and strawberries are grown seasonally by locals on the farmland. In the fall, the farm was filled with eight-foot-tall cornstalks. "It was so scenic that students decided that the library area with a view of the farm was a popular spot."

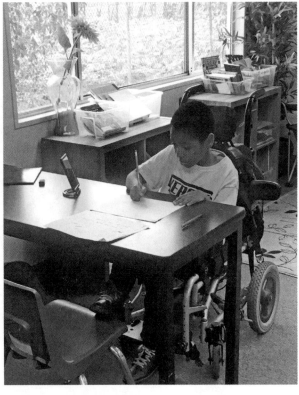

Color

Jamaica chose to use mostly neutral tones to design the look of the space so that everything felt spacious, calm, and connected. She used yellow, orange, and darker blues to accent or spark interest in particular areas.

Sound

To reduce the noise that often makes learning tasks and concentration more difficult, Jamaica employed a few strategies. One was shoeless learning.

"I let my students know that working in socks is an option. It can help keep things quieter and feel more comfortable as they work. Many love it."

Another strategy was the use of fabrics.

"In addition to our carpeted floor, I purchased pillows, table coverings, placemats, and other furnishings that help decrease reverberation and dampen sound around the classroom."

Natural Elements

Jamaica used both real and artificial plants and trees around the classroom.

Students were encouraged to collect and bring in nature items to share, discuss, tell stories about, and to add to a counting collection. They brought in rocks, shells, pebbles, branches, leaves, and an occasional dead insect.

Care and Maintenance

Everyone pitched in to help with classroom cleaning rituals by rotating through assigned areas in partnerships.

"I take responsibility for cleaning up my own personal materials. We operate under the concept that everything has a place and at the end of a learning period and at the end of the day, we restore the space to the way it was when we walked in that morning. It has worked well."

WORKS CITED

Abdelbary, Marwa. 2017. "Learning in Motion: Bring Movement Back to the Classroom." *Education Week Teacher*, August 9. www.edweek.org/tm/articles/2017/08/08/learning-in-motion-bring-movement-back-to.html.

Abramson, Paul. 2015. "Measuring Elementary School Capacity." *School Planning and Management*, December 1. https://webspm.com/Articles/2015/12/01/School-Capacity.aspx.

Barrett, Peter. 2013. "The Small Changes in Classroom Environment That Can Improve Learning." *The Guardian*, April 25. www.theguardian.com/teacher-network/2013/apr/25/changing-classroom-environment-improve-learning.

Barrett, Peter, Fay Davies, Yufan Zhang, and Lucinda Barrett. 2015. "The Impact of Classroom Design on Pupils' Learning: Final Results of a Holistic, Multi-Level Analysis." *Building and Environment* 89: 118–33. doi:10.1016/j.buildenv.2015.02.013.

Brooks, D. Christopher. 2011. "Space Matters: The Impact of Formal Learning Environments on Student Learning." *British Journal of Educational Technology* 42 (5): 719–26.

Burden, Paul R. 2003. *Classroom Management: Creating a Successful Learning Community.* 2nd ed. New York: John Wiley.

Calkins, Lucy. 2003. *The Nuts and Bolts of Teaching Writing.* Portsmouth, NH: FirstHand.

Cangelosi, James S. 2000. *Classroom Management Strategies: Gaining and Maintaining Students' Cooperation.* 4th ed. New York: John Wiley.

Cheryan, Sapna, Sianna A. Ziegler, Victoria C. Plaut, and Andrew N. Meltzoff. 2014. "Designing Classrooms to Maximize Student Achievement." *Policy Insights from the Behavioral and Brain Sciences* 1 (1): 4–12. doi:10.1177/2372732214548677.

Clifford, Miriam. 2012. "Learning Environment: 20 Things Educators Need to Know About Learning Spaces." *InformED* (blog), September 29. www.opencolleges.edu.au/informed/features/20-things-educators-need-to-know-about-learning-spaces/.

Danielson, Charlotte. 2015. *The Framework for Teaching Evaluation Instrument.* Cheltenham, Victoria, Australia: Hawker Brownlow Education.

Edwards, L., and P. Torcelli. 2002. *A Literature Review of the Effects of Natural Light on Building Occupants.* Golden, CO: National Renewable Energy Laboratory.

Engelbrecht, Kathie. 2003. *The Impact of Color on Learning.* Chicago: Perkins and Will. www.semanticscholar.org/paper/The-Impact-of-Color-on-Learning-Engelbrecht/370a5af3c86c1255defe3a1e83a13e9950958800.

Fielding, Randall. 2006. "Learning, Lighting and Color: Lighting Design for Schools and Universities in the 21st Century." DesignShare. https://designshare.com/articles/1/133/fielding_light-learn-color.pdf.

Friedlander, Jamie. 2018. "Tony Robbins' Secrets for Effective Goal Setting." *Success*, December 4. www.success.com/tony-robbins-goals/.

Fromberg, Doris P., and Maryanne Driscoll. 1985. *The Successful Classroom: Management Strategies for Regular and Special Education Teachers.* New York: Teachers College Press.

Greenman, Jim. 1988. *Caring Spaces, Learning Places: Children's Environments That Work.* Redmond, WA: Exchange Press.

Grossman, Randi P., and Joseph Z. Wisenblit. 1999. "What We Know About Consumers' Color Choices." *Journal of Marketing Practice* 5 (3): 78–90.

Hammond, Zaretta, and Yvette Jackson. 2015. *Culturally Responsive Teaching and the Brain: Promoting Authentic Engagement and Rigor Among Culturally and Linguistically Diverse Students*. Thousand Oaks, CA: Corwin.

Hare, Rebecca Louise, and Robert Dillon. 2016. *The Space: A Guide for Educators*. Irvine, CA: EdTechTeam.

Harmon, William. 1979. *The Oxford Book of American Light Verse*. Oxford, United Kingdom: Oxford University Press.

Heppell, Stephen J. 2011. "Shoeless Learning Spaces." Heppell.net. http://rubble.heppell.net/places/shoeless/default.html.

Heppell, Stephen, Juliette Heppell, and Melissa Heppell. 2015. "Agile Learning Spaces: A User Manual for Teachers and Students." Heppell.net. http://rubble.heppell.net/media_forum/wesley_spaces2.pdf.

Kang, Sean H. K. 2016. "Spaced Repetition Promotes Efficient and Effective Learning." *Policy Insights from the Behavioral and Brain Sciences* 3 (1): 12–19.

Kaplan, Rachel, and Stephen Kaplan. 1989. *The Experience of Nature: A Psychological Perspective*. New York: Cambridge University Press.

Kliever, Janie. 2016. "The 9 Graphic Design Trends You Need to Be Aware of in 2016." *Canva Design* (blog). www.canva.com/learn/design-trends-2016/.

Lishcher, Brian. 2018. "The Psychology of Color in Branding." *Ignyte Blog*. www.ignytebrands.com/the-psychology-of-color-in-branding/.

Markant, Douglas, Azzurra Ruggeri, Todd M. Gureckis, and Fei Xu. 2016. "Enhanced Memory as a Common Effect of Active Learning." *Mind, Brain, and Education* 10 (3): 142–52.

Martinez, Sylvia L., and Gary Stager. 2013. *Invent to Learn: Making, Tinkering, and Engineering in the Classroom*. Torrance, CA: Constructing Modern Knowledge.

Marzano, Robert J., Debra Pickering, and Jane E. Pollock. 2001. *Classroom Instruction That Works: Research-Based Strategies for Increasing Student Achievement*. Alexandria, VA: ASCD.

McCormick, Rachel. 2017. "Does Access to Green Space Impact the Mental Well-Being of Children: A Systematic Review." *Journal of Pediatric Nursing* 37: 3–7.

National Research Council Committee to Review and Assess the Health and Productivity Benefits of Green Schools. 2007. Green Schools: *Attributes for Health and Learning*. Washington, DC: National Academies Press.

Olson, Judy L., and Jennifer M. Platt. 2000. *Teaching Children and Adolescents with Special Needs*. 3rd ed. Upper Saddle River, NJ: Merrill.

Parrett, William H., and Kathleen M. Budge. 2012. *Turning High-Poverty Schools into High-Performing Schools*. Alexandria, VA: ASCD.

Proust, Marcel. 2003. *In Search of Lost Time*. Trans. by Ian Patterson. Penguin.

Rankin, Baji. 2004. "The Importance of Intentional Socialization Among Children in Small Groups: A Conversation with Loris Malaguzzi." *Early Childhood Education Journal* 32 (2): 81–85.

Rohrer, Marcia, and Nannette Samson. 2014. *10 Critical Components for Success in the Special Education Classroom*. Thousand Oaks, CA: Corwin.

Rosenberg, Michael S., Rich Wilson, Larry Maheady, and Paul T. Sindelar. 1997. *Educating Students with Behavior Disorders*. 2nd ed. Boston: Allyn and Bacon.

Rosenthal, R., and Lenore Jacobson. 2003. *Pygmalion in the Classroom: Teacher Expectation and Pupils' Intellectual Development*. Norwalk, CT: Crown House.

Sainato, Diane M. 1990. "Classroom Transitions: Organizing Environments to Promote Independent Performance in Preschool Children with Disabilities." *Education and Treatment of Children* 13 (4): 288–97.

Scott, Katy. 2010. "Let Them Tinker." *Stretch Your Digital Dollar* (blog), April 19. https://digitaldollar. edublogs.org/2010/04/19/let-them-tinker/.

Sibley, Benjamin A., and Jennifer L. Etnier. 2003. "The Relationship Between Physical Activity and Cognition in Children: A Meta-Analysis." *Pediatric Exercise Science* 15 (3): 243–56.

Smith, Tom E. C., Edward A. Polloway, James R. Patton, and Carol A. Dowdy. 2001. *Teaching Students with Special Needs in Inclusive Settings*. 3rd ed. Boston: Allyn and Bacon.

Stainback, Susan, and William Stainback. 1996. *Inclusion: A Guide for Educators*. Baltimore: Paul H. Brookes.

Stenger, Marianne. 2014. "Why Curiosity Enhances Learning." *Edutopia* (blog), December 17. https://www. edutopia.org/blog/why-curiosity-enhances-learning-marianne-stenger.

Stronge, James H., and Jennifer L. Hindman. 2003. "Hiring the Best Teachers." *Educational Leadership* 60 (8): 48–52.

Stronge, James H., Pamela D. Tucker, and Jennifer L. Hindman. 2004. *Handbook for Qualities of Effective Teachers*. Alexandria, VA: ASCD.

Tanner, C. Kenneth. 2008. "Explaining Relationships Among Student Outcomes and the School's Environment." *Journal of Advanced Academics* 19 (3): 444–71.

———. 2009. "Effects of School Design on Student Outcomes." *Journal of Educational Administration* 47: 381–99.

Troncoso, Xoana G., Stephen L. Macknik, and Susana Martinez-Conde. 2005. "Novel Visual Illusions Related to Vasarely's 'Nested Squares' Show That Corner Salience Varies with Corner Angle." *Perception* 34 (4): 409–20.

———. 2009. "Corner Salience Varies Linearly with Corner Angle During Flicker-Augmented Contrast: A General Principle of Corner Perception Based on Vasarely's Artworks." *Spatial Vision* 22 (3): 211–24.

Troncoso, Xoana G., Peter U. Tse, Stephen L. Macknik, Gideon P. Caplovitz, Po-Jang Hsieh, Alexander A. Schlegel, Jorge Otero-Millan, and Susana Martinez-Conde. 2007. "BOLD Activation Varies Parametrically with Corner Angle Throughout Human Retinotopic Cortex." *Perception* 36 (6): 808–11.

Ulrich, Roger. 1984. "View Through a Window May Influence Recovery from Surgery." *Science* 224 (4647): 420–21. doi:10.1126/science.6143402.

Vartuli, Sue, and Carol Phelps. 1980. "Classroom Transitions." *Childhood Education* 57 (2): 94–96.

Wang, Margaret C., Geneva D. Haertel, and Herbert J. Walberg. 1993/1994. "Synthesis of Research/What Helps Students Learn?" *Educational Leadership* 51 (4): 74–79.

Wells, Nancy M. 2000. "At Home with Nature: Effects of 'Greenness' on Children's Cognitive Functioning." *Environment and Behavior* 32 (6): 775–95.

Willis, Judy. 2006. *Research-Based Strategies to Ignite Student Learning: Insights from a Neurologist and Classroom Teacher*. Alexandria, VA: ASCD.

———. 2018. "Applying Learning in Multiple Contexts." *Edutopia*, November 30. www.edutopia.org/article/ applying-learning-multiple-contexts.

Wilson, Bruce L., and H. Dickson Corbett. 1999. *"No Excuses": The Eighth Grade Year in Six Philadelphia Middle Schools*. Philadelphia: Philadelphia Education Fund.

Wilson, Donna. 2014. "Move Your Body, Grow Your Brain." *Edutopia*, March 12. www.edutopia.org/blog/ move-body-grow-brain-donna-wilson.

Wolchover, Natalie. 2012. "Why Do We Have Personal Space?" *LiveScience*, June 6. www.livescience. com/20801-personal-space.html.

Xu, Alison Jing, and Aparna A. Labroo. 2014. "Incandescent Affect: Turning on the Hot Emotional System with Bright Light." *Journal of Consumer Psychology* 24 (2): 207–16. doi:10.1016/j.jcps.2013.12.007.